DOCKLANDS HERITAGE

C

DOCKLANDS HERITAGE
CONSERVATION AND REGENERATION IN LONDON DOCKLANDS

PUBLISHED BY LONDON DOCKLANDS DEVELOPMENT CORPORATION

First published in 1987
by LONDON DOCKLANDS DEVELOPMENT CORPORATION
Thames House, Basin South, London E16 2QY

© London Docklands Development Corporation

CONSULTANT EDITOR, Edward Hollamby, OBE

EDITORS, Carole Lyders, Averil Harrison

RESEARCH, Edward Sargent

DESIGN, Colin Dunne

PRODUCTION, Geoff Nyburg

PROJECT DIRECTOR, David Morgan

TYPESET in Sabon 9K on 11·5F by Plus Five Limited.

COLOUR SEPARATED IN DOCKLANDS by Magic Reprographics Limited.

PRINTED IN DOCKLANDS by M J Horrigan Limited

ISBN 0 9509877 3 5

Contents

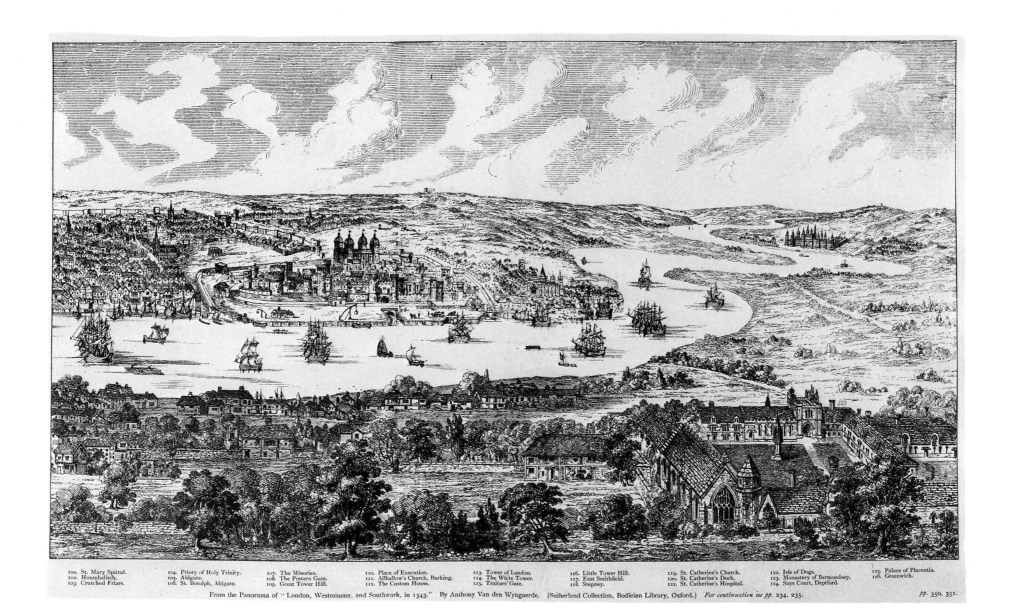

From the Panorama of " London, Westminster, and Southwark, in 1543." By Anthony Van den Wyngaerde. (Sutherland Collection, Bodleian Library, Oxford.) *For continuation see pp. 234, 235.*

pp. 350, 351.

Foreword

The London Docklands Development Corporation, established under the provisions of the Local Government, Planning and Land Act 1980, is charged with the regeneration of East London.

In its first six years the Corporation has brought about enormous environmental changes within its area, predominantly through new development.

From the outset, however, conservation has been seen by the Corporation as playing a major, constructive role in its regeneration policies and programmes by contributing to the improvement of Docklands' environment, by providing the very best development and refurbishment opportunities and by helping in first establishing and then maintaining the reputation of Docklands as an 'exceptional place.'

This has been recognised by the Heritage Trust which is staging an international congress in London in 1987, a component of which is to be an exhibition in Docklands in April.

This Corporation publication celebrates the part which conservation of the Docklands Heritage has played in six years of regeneration. It gives the context within which policies and actions are being pursued and the opportunities these create for the enjoyment of Docklands' unique heritage.

The IDLE 'PRENTICE turn'd away, and sent to Sea.

Proverbs CHAP: X. Ve: 1.
A Foolish Son is the heaviness
of his Mother.

Design'd & Engrav'd by Wᵐ Hogarth

Plate 5.

Publish'd according to Act of Parliamᵗ Sep 30 1747.

'The Idle Prentice turned away and sent to sea' published by Hogarth in 1747, shows the windmills along the western side of the Isle of Dogs from which Millwall takes it's name. The engraving shows the actual site of the local gibbet on which common criminals were left to hang as a warning to others.

Introduction

The economic and social history of a country is reflected in its buildings and in the way its people have shaped their environment to meet their needs. Today's built environment is the product of the accumulated impact of society's activities on its natural and man-made surroundings.

Some periods in history have brought dramatic social and economic changes which have transformed those surroundings. Such transformations have sometimes been beneficial – as with the changes to agriculture and the English landscape of the 18th Century. But more often than not they have been catastrophic to the physical environment, and in particular to the heritage represented by its architecture, its monuments and its art.

The 20th Century, which has contributed its share of the destruction of that heritage, has also seen changes in man's attitude to history and to the built environment he has inherited. John Ruskin and William Morris had pointed the way in the 19th Century; the Society for the Protection of Ancient Buildings, founded by Morris, Philip Webb and others in 1877 (its first meeting was attended by the philosopher James Carlisle as well as Ruskin) established an attitude to historic buildings that is still relevant today. In the period since, bodies such as The National Trust, The Civic Trust, and a multitude of environmental and civic societies, have emerged to educate, guide and articulate public awareness of the significance to civilised life of the physical environment, and in particular to value what history has bequeathed in architecture, landscape and art.

However, despite changes in public opinion over the years, there are still in some quarters strongly held views and powerful voices which see protection and conservation as barriers to development and change. This need not, and indeed should not, be so. The regeneration of London Docklands was initiated primarily for economic and social reasons, but it creates a unique opportunity to conserve and enjoy the physical heritage, to retain the magnificence of the vast dock water systems, to invigorate the older urban fabric with new activity and to enhance the character of the best of it and thereby to establish an ambience which is special, which breathes 'the spirit of the place.' Regeneration also demands high quality of the new: it requires that a heritage is enriched by the changes that have been wrought on it, so that it in turn becomes a heritage that future generations will want to conserve and protect.

The London Docklands Development Corporation, established in 1980 to bring about the regeneration of East London, realised it had inherited an area of great opportunity and above all a unique place. It took the view from the outset that surviving elements of the past should, wherever practicable, be retained and absorbed into the massive development effort, to contribute to the framework for permanent regeneration and to provide the 'new Docklands' with a continuing link between past and future. This view of conservation was consistent with the LDDC's purpose and role and with a philosophy which saw conservation itself as an agent of change, reflecting the unique history and character of Docklands.

In some of the older areas of Docklands – Wapping, Limehouse, Bermondsey and Rotherhithe – the regeneration that is taking place is conservation led.

Elsewhere – and particularly in East Docklands and the Surrey Docks – conservation planning has meant protection of the surviving fragments of history. In the Isle of Dogs, with its Enterprise Zone, new development has taken the dominant role, tempered by an understanding of the history of the area, its topography, waterscape and remaining artefacts – both architectural and engineering.

Throughout the area, however, the conservation of the Docklands heritage is a key part of the LDDC's regeneration strategy. The conservation of individual historic buildings provides attractive space for new activities and homes for residents, while providing an interesting framework for new developments. A positive planning policy that encourages the conservation of worthwhile old buildings for suitable new uses is now eradicating the dereliction caused in many historic areas by empty buildings and low grade uses. At the same time derelict sites adjacent to historic buildings are being brought back into use as the areas become more attractive. The designation of conservation areas has provided the means of retaining the character of historic areas and ensuring that new buildings within them respect their surroundings. The conservation of the docks themselves and the introduction of historic vessels provide evocative and exciting settings for new developments.

The heritage of Docklands is a powerful draw for those who have the responsibility to choose new investment and business locations, for those who decide to make their homes and to work there, for those who visit and enjoy its attractions, and not least for those deeply rooted traditional communities who take pride in its past. Its successful conservation will ensure that Docklands indeed can retain its reputation as an 'exceptional place.'

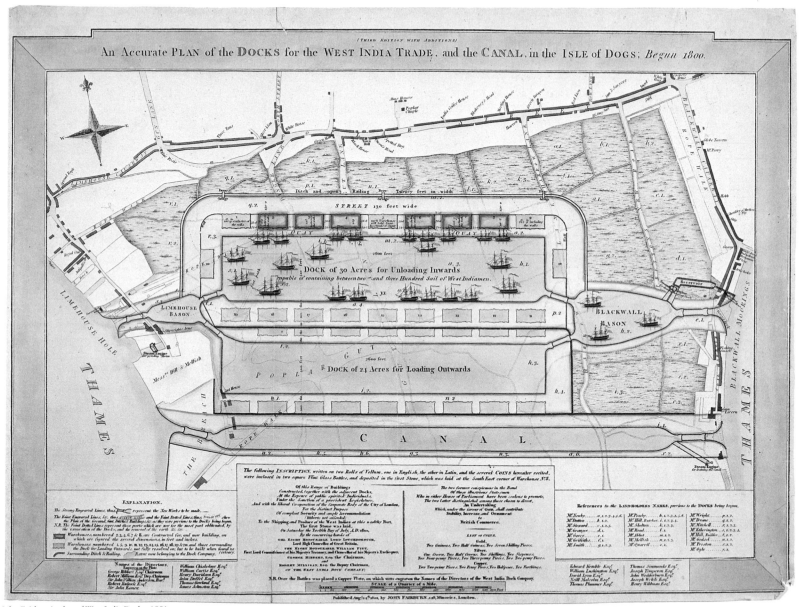

John Fairburn's plan of West India Docks, 1801.

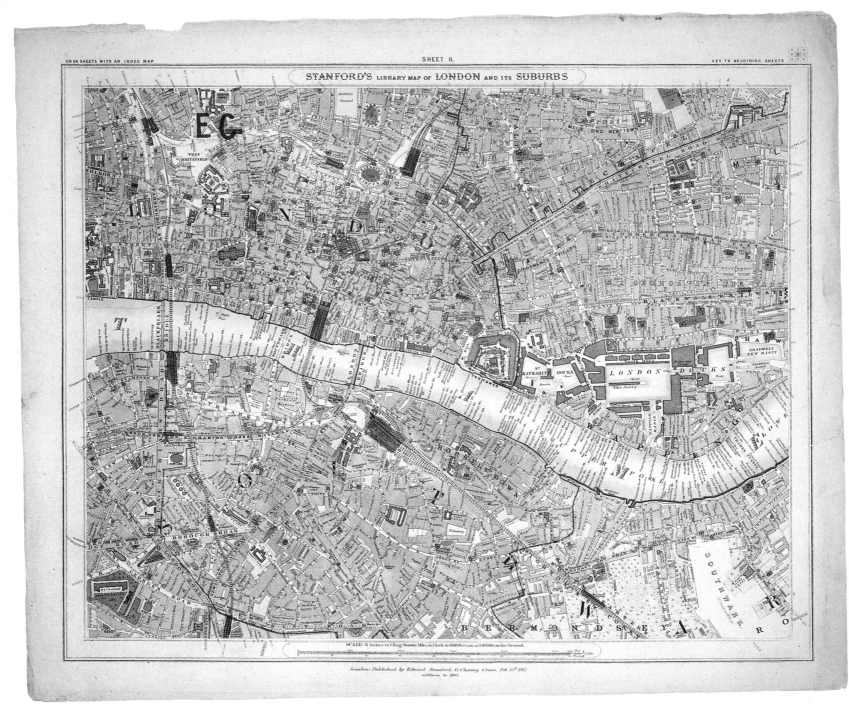

Sheet 2 from Stanford's Map of London, 1865 showing the location of the now infilled London Docks.

The History of London Docklands

Docklands lies predominantly within the flood plain of the lower Thames and its tributaries. The Southwark riverside, the Isle of Dogs, the Lower Lea Valley and Beckton originally consisted of riverside marshland and rough grazing before the massive engineering projects in the 19th Century, created by the development of the Port of London, converted much of them into the vast and intricate commercial dock system that thrived for a century or more.

The Port of London developed to provide the merchant and later the banking and insurance economy of the City of London with its trade with the world. The Port and the City spawned industry and manufacture and the process developed by which East London and Docklands became, literally, the 'back yard' of London.

Successive waves of immigrants brought their trades with them, providing the workforce for the new industries. In the 16th Century London's economy first developed through the wool and cloth trades. With the growth of the Port and the enclosed docks in the 19th Century, East London became the 'Enterprise Zone' of the capital, with shipbuilding, engineering, chemicals, furniture and clothing manufacture, brewing and other industries.

The work people lived in appalling conditions of overcrowding and squalor, cheek by jowl with polluting and unhealthy factories, yards and workshops. Cholera was endemic. In spite of improvements in public health legislation, the East End remained congested, overcrowded and unhealthy into the 20th Century, alongside a teeming river and a port of modern enclosed docks, bursting with trade with the world. Indeed, it was at

The Royal Mint

The Match Girls, c1888

the interface between the City and the docks that the Royal Mint was established, its handsome façade symbolically directed towards the City and its back to East London.

The latter end of the 19th Century saw the development of organised labour. The names of the men and women who articulated and led gas workers, dockers and the famous 'Match Girls' in struggles that were as much against appalling working conditions as for economic advancement, still reverberate around Docklands and the East End: names like John Burns, a future Minister of Health; Will Thorne, still illiterate when a grown man and taught to read and write by Karl Marx's daughter, Eleanor; Ben Tillett, circus boy and docker who led the great strike for the 'Dockers' Tanner' in 1888; and Tom Mann and Annie Besant, wife of the writer Sir Walter Besant who helped to establish the 'People's Palace' in the Mile End Road.

At the same time the conditions of poverty and even degradation endured by many of the families of these workers inspired a diverse band of social workers and reformers to work among them and attempt to alleviate their conditions. Names like Samuel and Henrietta Barnett, later of Hampstead Garden Suburb fame, and Arnold Toynbee and Charles Booth, together with others less well known, have faded into the social history of East London. The institutions they founded – The Docklands Settlement, Toynbee Hall, The Whitechapel Art Gallery and The Workers' Educational Association, became centres of self-help, where East End workers could pull themselves up by their bootlaces through education and knowledge. John Ruskin and William Morris lectured at the Working Men's Institutes and the philanthropist Passmore Edwards built public libraries. Slowly a new type of educated workman emerged from the mass of immigrants and illiterate labourers.

The Docks and Their Decline

It was, however, the creation of two public bodies that was to have the greatest impact on the East End and

Docklands. In 1888 the London County Council (LCC) was established and in 1908 the Port of London Authority (PLA). The LCC's role was, at first, to provide municipal services such as education, housing, health and the fire service, although it was restricted, under the terms of its establishment by central Government, in the powers that it had. For example it was not responsible for water supply: the two great main drainage schemes for London had been initiated by the old Metropolitan Board of Works, whose responsibility for London's water supply was taken over by the Metropolitan Water Board, established in 1902. It was in slum clearance and housing, and later in planning, that the LCC made its greatest contribution. The most direct impact on Docklands and its physical and economic condition was provided by the PLA. A thirty-foot channel, one thousand feet wide, was dredged by the PLA through the fifty miles of river from London Bridge to the sea, to allow the ocean-going vessels of the 20th Century to penetrate to the heart of London. In a massive programme of constructing and reconstructing docks, wharves and warehouses the PLA and its forceful chairman Lord Davenport put the docks on a new footing (though it must be said that the architectural and engineering results of all this effort seldom rose to the occasion in the way that the great dock buildings of the 19th Century had). Nevertheless, in 1939 the PLA could celebrate its thirtieth birthday and its apparent success in transforming London's dock system by doubling the value of trade passing through it annually and increasing its volume from under 40 million to 60 million tons. The PLA could well justify the apparent wealth and optimism – not to mention the whiff of imperial greatness – expressed in the exciting and beautiful documentary 'City of Ships' which it commissioned.

But it was the calm before the storm. In the summer of 1940 the Port and East London took the brunt of the Luftwaffe's massive aerial onslaught on the metropolis. Arthur Bryant's 'Liquid History' quotes Sir Alan Herbert's vivid description of the scene of the conflagration on the evening of September 7th as like '*a lake in hell*,' the like of which had not been seen since the Great Fire of 1666. For over two months the Port and East London were under nightly bombardment.

The widespread destruction of the docks and the devastation of the streets of East London had resulted in a huge reduction of the population by the end of the war. The London County Council was determined to see the resurrection of the East End as a model of a planned, efficient and beautiful London. Equipped with the town planning powers it obtained under post-war legislation, and with the Abercrombie/Forshaw County of London Plan of 1944 as its bible, it prepared a far-reaching reconstruction plan for its Stepney/Poplar Comprehensive Development Area. The neighbourhood of Lansbury was built as a model neighbourhood for the 1951 Festival of Britain. However, it is worth noting that neither Abercrombie's imaginative 1944 plan nor the LCC's more prosaic Statutory Development Plan of 1951 had anything to say about conservation, and concern for historic buildings went no further than an acceptance of the duty to preserve a handful of religious and secular buildings.

The future of the docks themselves was never questioned, and this is understandable when their remarkable recovery after the war is examined. By 1959 the tonnage handled by the Port, which had fallen to less than 40 million tons by the end of the war, had risen to over 50 million tons annually, and the PLA had virtually completed its post-war reconstruction of the docks. London's five vast dock groups now handled a third of all Britain's seaborne trade.

But the optimism of the early 1950s was illusory. In spite of the massive housing drive by the LCC in building huge estates on the suburban/rural periphery of London, and the Government's even more significant programme for the construction of new towns around London, the great reconstruction plans for East London could not proceed quickly enough for their 'Brave New World' image

to succeed; and it was only in the late 1950s in South London that the LCC discovered the logistic as well as architectural virtues of rehabilitation and conservation. So conservation was conspicuously absent from the LCC's planned renaissance of the East End. Meanwhile the apparent economic recovery of the docks faltered and they entered into a period of rapid and terminal decline, the effects of which were economically and socially catastrophic. Historically and physically cut off from the mainstream of London life, hidden behind high brick walls, overshadowed by the achievements of the adjacent City of London, and cold-shouldered as the capital spread westwards, the docks themselves – the economic foundation of great parts of East London, were to close.

One last effort to halt the decline of the area was made in the form of a Joint Committee of the Greater London Council and five riparian boroughs which in the mid-1970s produced its Strategic Plan for Docklands. Prior to the setting up of the Joint Committee the Government had commissioned planning consultants Travers Morgan to study development options for the East End. They offered a choice of five planning modes: Europa, Thames Park, City New Town, Waterside and East End Consolidated. Perhaps inevitably it was East End Consolidated that bore the closest resemblance to the Joint Committee's Strategic Plan. The shrinking docks, to be used as new housing areas for East End residents, were to allow the East End to spread, but not to change.

Thus both wartime bombing and the socially rigid formulae of the 'Brave New World' redevelopment contributed to the catastrophic collapse of the East London economy. Conscious policies of removing 'non-conforming' industries from residential areas made the local economy even more dependent on the employment and trading capacity of the docks – and they also moved. With the changing economics of cargo handling, the container revolution led to the removal of the Port to Tilbury and the progressive closure of the whole of the London dock system.

Luftwaffe over Docklands

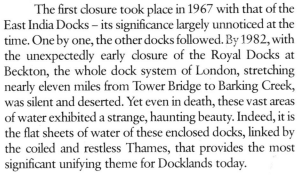

West India Docks   Limehouse Basin Viaduct

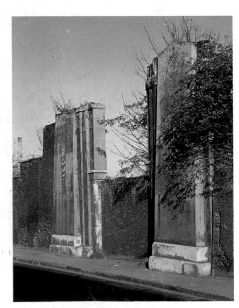

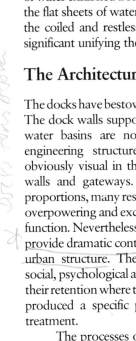

Gateway to the East India Company's Blackwall Warehouses   Coade Stone Detail

The first closure took place in 1967 with that of the East India Docks – its significance largely unnoticed at the time. One by one, the other docks followed. By 1982, with the unexpectedly early closure of the Royal Docks at Beckton, the whole dock system of London, stretching nearly eleven miles from Tower Bridge to Barking Creek, was silent and deserted. Yet even in death, these vast areas of water exhibited a strange, haunting beauty. Indeed, it is the flat sheets of water of these enclosed docks, linked by the coiled and restless Thames, that provides the most significant unifying theme for Docklands today.

The Architectural Heritage

The docks have bestowed a distinctive architectural legacy. The dock walls supporting the quays and containing the water basins are now recognised for the important engineering structures that they are. Perhaps more obviously visual in their impact are the dock boundary walls and gateways. Despite their splendidly massive proportions, many residents and some visitors see these as overpowering and excluding – as indeed was their historic function. Nevertheless, many of these walls are listed and provide dramatic contrasts of scale and texture within the urban structure. The Corporation has recognised the social, psychological and environmental issues involved in their retention where they are of architectural value and has produced a specific policy document concerning their treatment.

The processes of dock construction fundamentally altered existing drainage patterns, replacing them with new hydraulic operations. New land ownerships and uses were established, and an essentially man-made environment based upon a new and developing technology was created in flat marshlands. The system of dock entrances, impounded water areas, canals and mudchutes, as well as many of the artefacts associated with port activities, remain throughout much of Docklands with the exception of those areas which were filled in during the 1970s. Indeed at Beckton it was not until 1977 that the marshes north of the Royal Docks were drained.

The river itself has been progressively walled and contained, both to prevent flooding and to provide wharfage along the river banks. Some of these walls and dock entrances (as at Greenland and South Docks) are listed and protected, but for the most part are of utilitarian construction, protected with jetties, piles and timber whalings. Often irregular and indented in this way, the river walls have a characteristic waterside flavour which needs to be retained. At St. Saviour's Dock the deep penetration of the existing shoreline indicates the original location of the River Neckinger, one of the many local rivers which fed into the Thames close to central London.

Because shipping and road transport could not be disrupted, crossing the river east of London Bridge has in the past been by tunnelled routes, with the exception of one of London's greatest architectural treasures – Tower Bridge. This great structure still dominates its surroundings and provides a splendid western gateway to Docklands as well as an architectural frame to the City and central London.

Rail transport has also left its mark. The railway viaduct – an engineering structure of considerable historical and visual significance – is an archetypal form of the 19th Century: contemporary lithographs show them striding across the marshes. Alas, the arches of most of London's railway viaducts have been filled in and London and its suburban growth has engulfed them. However, at Limehouse Basin, and the open space of Millwall Park in the Isle of Dogs, something of their former character remains to come to life again supporting the track of the new Docklands Railway, which will also exhibit in modern form the visual excitement of viaduct structures. The London and Blackwall Railway, opened in 1840, was probably the first rapid transit system in the world. Designed to take passengers from London to the steamers at Brunswick Wharf, it was originally rope hauled and the time from London to Blackwall was only 13 minutes.

Significantly, it was the first public railway to use the electric telegraph. It is fitting, therefore, that the new railway, using the latest technology, should be carried over the viaduct of a railway which used technology that in its day was equally advanced.

Docklands' Historic Neighbours

However, Docklands is not a self contained island, but an integral part of east and south east London. The LDDC's boundaries – stretching from London Bridge to Deptford on the southern side of the Thames, and from Tower Bridge to Beckton on the opposite bank, are a purely administrative invention overlaid upon the physical structure of the area. It is not surprising therefore that a number of important places whose history has been closely bound up with the development of the Port of London and Docklands lie outside its boundaries.

Spitalfields, Whitechapel and Petticoat Lane lie to the north of the LDDC's boundaries in Tower Hamlets. The old Royal Mint, which now forms part of an adjacent conservation area, shared its boundary with the St. Katharine Docks along East Smithfield. On the south side of the river was the famous naval victualling yard at Deptford: visited by Peter the Great in 1698, it also contained the house in which Samuel Pepys lived when he served as Secretary to the Admiralty.

Round the bend of the river and directly opposite the viewing point of Island Gardens at the southern tip of the Isle of Dogs is the magnificent panorama of Greenwich Palace. Still further east are Woolwich and the Royal Arsenal, and fragments of the old Woolwich naval dockyard, where the 'Great Harry' (1512) and the 'Royal Sovereign' (1637) were built.

But it is on the northern side of the Thames at St. James' Ratcliffe that there lies an extraordinary and little known survival of what has been described as an 'urban oasis,' in the form of the Royal Foundation of St. Katharine. Although just outside the LDDC boundary the

Canaletto's 'View of Greenwich Palace'

Railway Viaduct, Millwall Park

Foundation is of great importance to Docklands for environmental, social and historic reasons.

The Foundation's history and community work are described in detail in the section of this book dealing with Docklands' historic buildings and structures, as are the architectural and historic features of Docklands' many churches, public and industrial buildings and dock and riverside structures and the work being undertaken today to protect them.

Royal Foundation of St. Katharine, Wall Paintings by an Unknown Artist

Protecting the Heritage

Government action to protect historic buildings commenced with the Ancient Monuments Protection Act of 1882. The concept of protecting buildings in everyday use, as distinct from ecclesiastical buildings and disused monuments such as castles, ruins and burial sites, is more recent.

The first such Act in 1932 gave local authorities the power to make preservation orders, but it was only in 1944 that the Town and Country Planning Act gave the Minister the power to prepare lists of buildings of special architectural or historic interest and in 1947 the duty to prepare such lists. The 1968 and 1971 Town and Country Planning Acts introduced the concept of 'Listed Building Consent', requiring express permission to alter or demolish in whole or in part a listed historic building.

At the same time, Duncan Sandys' Civic Amenities Act of 1967 established the aesthetic and historic value of whole areas of buildings and the spaces which they enclose or which provide their setting. The concept of Conservation Areas, which may or may not contain listed buildings or scheduled monuments but which comprise *'areas of special architectural or historic interest, the character and appearance of which it is desirable to preserve or enhance,'* added a new dimension to the protection of historic buildings as part of the planning system of Britain.

The Secretary of State in Circular 23/1977, which deals with Government policy in relation to listed buildings and conservation areas, makes the importance of conservation and its contribution to the planning system crystal clear:

'Historic Buildings and Conservation Areas are vitally important to the environmental quality of life in this country. Buildings of architectural and historic merit should receive very special attention. Local authorities stand in the vanguard of those protecting historic buildings and areas, and the Secretary of State hopes they will make diligent use of all the powers available to them. Public opinion is now overwhelmingly in favour of conserving and enhancing the familiar and cherished local scene, and authorities should take account of this when framing their policies affecting Historic Buildings and Conservation Areas...'

More recently, the National Heritage Act of 1983 empowered the Secretary of State for the Environment to set up the Commission on Historic Buildings and Monuments, now known as English Heritage. The powers of this influential body were greatly extended in 1986, when it took over the former Greater London Council's responsibilities for historic buildings and conservation in London.

The LDDC's Approach to Conservation and Regeneration

The powers and responsibilities of the London Docklands Development Corporation, as set out in the provisions of the Local Government Land and Planning Act 1980, are abundantly clear:

'The object of an Urban Development Corporation shall be to secure...regeneration...by bringing land <u>and buildings</u> into effective use...'

The Secretary of State for the Environment defined this task as the *'Permanent Regeneration of Docklands.'*

Thus regeneration in Docklands explicitly involves bringing into use obsolete buildings, including those of architectural or historic importance, and the protection and environmental enhancement of conservation areas. The Corporation was given the powers of a local planning authority to control development, and responsibilities to protect historic buildings and designate conservation areas. The Secretary of State also indicated to the Corporation that it should *'make known its own planning views by issuing policy statements, planning briefs or plans for all or parts of its area.'*

In discharging this duty, the Corporation has produced a range of Area Development Strategies or Frameworks, Design Guides and Policy Statements covering such subjects as landscape strategy, access to the river and water areas, and dock enclosing walls. The setting out of its policies on conservation and historic buildings in the following pages represents a further step in this process.

Foremost amongst the planning issues facing the Corporation was the treatment of the water areas of the enclosed docks. Prior to the establishment of the LDDC it had been accepted by the Port of London Authority and the local authorities that such areas should be filled in to increase the land area available for development. However, not only was such land expensive to create, but the very process involved the destruction of Docklands' greatest single environmental asset. The Corporation realised that, far from being a liability, the areas of dock water were a great asset for that 'permanent regeneration' it was charged to create.

The vast open areas of dock water, with their long vistas and beautiful effects of light, offered superb settings for new, high quality buildings and gave the Corporation the opportunity to create an attractive environment for the new and existing populations of Docklands. Their effect has been enhanced in a number of cases by building out on piles over the water, recreating the modelling of the space formerly achieved by the lines of ships moored along the quay edges, in which the reflections on the water are a very important element.

The Corporation's decision to retain the water areas has since won overwhelming approval for aesthetic, historic and regenerative reasons. It has moreover created values in both financial and cultural terms.

Implicit in this conservation policy was the retention and protection of the dock walls themselves, some of which are of architectural and historic importance and are listed. A fundamental and related planning policy, adopted by the Corporation from its inception, was that the river and the water areas of the enclosed docks should be made accessible to the public as major elements of visual and recreational open space.

One other major policy was established from the beginning. That was the desirability of constructing a new Docklands Railway to link the area with the City and central London and with the large populated areas to the north – but of constructing it in such a way that it would not be a major intrusion into the surrounding built-up area. It was realised that the disused viaduct of the former London and Blackwall Railway – a substantial section of which through Limehouse is listed – could help to provide an acceptable route for a new overground railway, while the cuttings and embankments towards Stratford to the north would provide similar advantages for the Poplar to Stratford route.

Development in Conservation Areas

The LDDC has powers to control development, to protect historic buildings and monuments and to designate and enhance conservation areas.

Six of the ten conservation areas which it inherited from the Borough Councils in July 1981 had been designated as 'outstanding' and of national importance by the Department of the Environment on the advice of the

Historic Buildings Council of England. Since 1981 the Corporation has extended two of these, has itself designated a further seven areas and is in the process of designating or considering more: all contain groups of buildings and associated landscape and waterscape of architectural, historical and environmental interest. As underlined by the Secretary of State for the Environment in Circular 12/1981 (Historic Buildings and Conservation Areas), such designations ensure a stable planning environment and enable landowners and developers to have confidence and reasonable certainty of the status of their land, building or interest. Equally importantly, they provide assurance to the public and to local communities that such areas will be protected, and that appropriate environmental improvements will be undertaken.

Circular 23/77 states – *Designation of a conservation area will...be only a preliminary action to preserve or enhance its appearance. The local authorities should adopt a positive scheme for each area at an early stage.* The Corporation's proposals for such environmental improvements have been set out in its Area Planning Strategies and Frameworks and in its Corporate Plan, which is updated annually.

The fact that an area within Docklands has been designated does not mean that changes (including new building and even demolition) will not be permitted; it does mean, however, that the area's special character has been recognised and that proposals for new building and/or the demolition of non-listed buildings must comply with environmental objectives. New buildings, alterations and extensions within conservation areas must be of a high standard of design and must make a positive contribution to the architectural character of the area. They need not necessarily be designed as pastiche, though that may sometimes be appropriate. On the contrary, the interest and vitality which modern architecture can contribute will be welcome. Far from being discouraged, there will be many cases where new building will be positively encouraged, as a means of filling gaps in street frontages,

completing the enclosure of urban spaces and helping to eradicate dereliction.

Existing buildings which are not in themselves listed often contribute to the overall character and environment of a conservation area. The protection of such buildings is most important and paragraph 25 of Circular 23/77 makes the reason for this clear:

> *'Many attractive streets or villages owe their character, not so much to buildings of great individual merit, but to the harmony produced by a whole range or complex of buildings. Such areas require...careful treatment when proposals for redevelopment are under consideration, even if redevelopment only replaces a building that is neither of great merit in itself nor is immediately adjacent to a listed building.'*

The Corporation, as planning authority, will be able to ensure that such buildings are not demolished: it may also be able to help with repairs to unlisted buildings within conservation areas by grants. (See Appendix 1.) Similarly, the Corporation will carry out environmental improvements (such as landscaping and the enhancement of roads and street furniture) and will continue to monitor other work which may have an impact on the environment. For example it is especially important that trees within conservation areas should not be felled or thoughtlessly or unskilfully pruned. If work on them is felt necessary or desirable by the owners or occupiers of land, the Corporation must be notified and permissions obtained before work is put in hand. The LDDC acts quickly in such cases and is able to give helpful advice.

Listed Buildings and Listed Building Consent

Although only a small proportion of the buildings and structures of Docklands are listed, they are among the most distinctive and most valued features of the built environment, providing physical evidence of the history of

the area. Listed structures within the area include not only buildings, but also items of street furniture such as bollards and lamps as well as dock walls, locks and other riverside features.

Listed buildings are buildings that have been included in the Statutory List of Buildings of Special Architectural and Historic Interest compiled by the Secretary of State for the Environment. Incorporation in the Statutory List makes it unlawful to demolish or alter such a building or structure without Listed Building Consent.

The criteria for listing cover four groups of building type:

1 all buildings built before 1700 which survive in anything like their original condition;

2 most buildings of between 1700 and 1840 (though selection is necessary);

3 buildings of definite quality and character built between 1840 and 1914; and

4 a limited number of buildings of high quality designed between 1914 and 1939.

Within the criteria for listing, buildings are subject to careful selection, and the more recent the building, the more selective the listing. With buildings of the late 19th and 20th Centuries, it is usually required that they be designed by an architect of note, or that they be of particular importance to the history of architecture.

Early in the life of the Corporation it was realised that the opening up of the dock areas would bring to light many buildings and structures which were likely to be listed when the Department of the Environment's periodic re-survey of East London was next carried out. To have had to wait for a re-survey to be done would have created great uncertainty for landowners, builders and the development industry, as well as involving the LDDC and Department of the Environment in an immense amount of spot-listing. The Corporation therefore requested the Department of the Environment to bring forward the date of its next re-survey and its updating of the list for Docklands. This was done, and an up-to-date list was confirmed by the Secretary of State in July 1983.

A re-listing survey aims to include all buildings of listable quality within the survey area and the Department of the Environment is usually reluctant to make further additions to the list for five years after the survey has been done. There will, however, inevitably be anomalies in a survey covering such a large area, and some buildings of importance will undoubtedly have been omitted from the Docklands list. If it is thought a building should be added to the list a very strong case has to be made, and evidence not available at the time of the re-survey must be brought forward. It should be noted, however, that by July 1987 only twelve months of the Department of the Environment's five year delay period will be left to run.

It is the Corporation's policy to refuse listed building consent for the demolition of listed buildings: generally, the Corporation prefers to encourage the conversion of buildings to suitable new uses, if this is necessary for their continuing existence. Where it is argued that a building is unusable for structural or economic reasons, or where its existence impedes a sought-after development, stringent tests will be applied to the validity of the reason for demolition being sought. Even if the Corporation is minded to grant consent for demolition, however, the final decision rests with the Secretary of State for the Environment, who will apply the national criteria on demolition of listed buildings after seeking the advice of English Heritage.

Similarly, alterations which would result in the loss of the historic character of a listed building will be resisted, unless it can be shown that these are essential for the reasonably beneficial use of the building.

Building owners are encouraged by the Corporation to restore historic features on listed buildings and to ensure their sympathetic repair using suitable materials, preferably with the aid of professional advisers who have experience of historic building work: this ensures that the work will be carried out to a high standard and assists the Corporation in dealing with applications for listed building consent. When appropriate the Corporation will enter into Section 52 Agreements with developers to ensure the restoration of historic buildings. Historic building grants and their application are described in detail at Appendix 1.

The LDDC will also act to ensure that neglected buildings are put into reasonable condition. In cases where owners neglect buildings to such an extent that their condition becomes seriously decayed, attempts will be made to persuade them to repair their buildings voluntarily. If these are unsuccessful, the Corporation will take action, using repairs notices or Section 101 notices as appropriate. (See Appendix 3.)

The Local List

To complement the statutory list of historic buildings in Docklands, the LDDC is currently preparing a non-statutory local list of minor historic buildings and artefacts of special local interest. Most of the entries on the local list will be non-listed buildings in conservation areas. A few will be borderline cases which might merit official spot-listing or the issue of Building Preservation Notices if there were any indication of an intent to demolish, and these will be separately identified. Because of the recent updating of the Statutory List, it is unlikely that there will be a large number of such entries, but buildings such as the Dock Offices at Surrey Docks, Millwall Fire Station, 'S' warehouse at the Royal Victoria Dock and No.3 Vine Lane (off Tooley Street) might well be placed in this category.

The local list will be published in due course to alert the public, developers and their architects to the Corporation's view that special consideration needs to be given to the retention of such buildings, particularly where they possess 'group value.'

Former Dock Manager's Office, Surrey Docks

The Statutory List of Buildings of Special Architectural and Historic Interest can be inspected at the Corporation's offices or those of the local Borough Councils. The local list, when published, will be available for inspection at the LDDC's Area Offices, at Borough Council offices and at local public libraries.

3 Vine Lane

Historic Buildings and Structures

St. George-in-the-East

The unique character and history of Docklands have left in their wake a variety of structures and buildings of historic interest. Foremost amongst these are its churches (some of which date from the 17th and 18th Centuries), its range of dock and riverside structures and its warehouses. A number of these are listed. The area also contains a number of listed industrial and public buildings, from hydraulic power stations to pubs and from shipbuilding yards to public libraries. In addition some unusual and interesting items of equipment, machinery and design have been uncovered by the Corporation and other developers during the course of restoration work.

The Churches

With the striking exceptions of Tower Bridge and the great set piece of Greenwich (best seen from the Isle of Dogs) Docklands has inherited few truly great architectural monuments from the past. It has, however, been more than fortunate with its legacy of magnificent churches, which include some of the finest buildings in Docklands.

From its earliest days the Corporation has considered these great architectural monuments to be of major visual and symbolic significance for the future of Docklands. Many of the churches are large and have serious structural problems to contend with which are beyond the means of the small congregations of churchgoers, and the Corporation has therefore initiated a major programme of repair, stone cleaning and landscaping, some of which is described in detail later. The churches are also an important centre of community life,

and the Corporation is assisting in the addition of community facilities where the need for these is proved. Even when declared redundant for ecclesiastical use, their splendid spatial and aesthetic qualities make these churches particularly suitable for use as museums and architectural interpretation centres, exhibition space for the visual arts, and auditoria for music and drama.

St. George-in-the-East, Wapping

Among the first projects carried out by the Corporation was the cleaning, repair and landscaping of St. George-in-the-East. This superb building, designed by Nicholas Hawksmoor, lies just north of the LDDC boundary adjacent to The Highway, one of the main routes into Docklands from the City. Because of its strategic location it was considered important to repair defective stonework, clean the building and improve its setting. This has been done with dramatic effect.

St. George-in-the-East was built as a result of an Act of Parliament passed in 1711 during the reign of Queen Anne, which permitted a tax on coal to raise the money to build fifty churches in or near London. It was dedicated in 1729 and cost £18,557.3s to build. Gutted in 1941 when the German air force fire-bombed Docklands, the exterior was restored as a shell. A church hall and rectory were built within the shell in 1960-64. Its churchyard, which was laid out as a public garden in 1886, contains the Raine Memorial to brewer Henry Raine who founded Raine's School (now in Arbour Square) in 1719. He died, aged 87, in 1732.

St. Anne's Church, Limehouse

St. Anne's Church in Limehouse, with its superb churchyard setting, is the major church of Docklands. Another 'coal church', and also designed by Nicholas Hawksmoor, it was built in 1712-30 and is a vast building of immense quality. Its enormous tower can be seen from most parts of Docklands west of the River Lea.

Unfortunately, the church had been allowed to decay over the years and externally presented a sad appearance. Realising its tremendous importance to the environment of Docklands, the LDDC has begun an ambitious four phase repair and cleaning programme to be carried out over a number of years. Phase 1, the cleaning and repair of the east end, is complete. Phase 2, currently on site, comprises the cleaning and repair of the nave and the insertion of new roof trusses within the existing roof space. This extremely elegant solution, which enables the existing roof trusses to be left in situ, is a very good example of high quality conservation techniques. Further phases of work will cover the cleaning and repair of the west end and the tower, and the underpinning of the tower, should this prove necessary.

The interior of St. Anne's was reconstructed by Philip Hardwick in 1851 following a fire. Its organ, built by Grey and Davidson, and installed at St. Anne's in 1851 shortly after winning the organ prize at the Great Exhibition, is one of the best surviving unaltered Victorian organs in the country. Apart from being fitted with an electric blower, it remains in its original form and is capable of producing high quality performances of 19th Century organ music. The organ is now in need of repair, and the Corporation would wish to give encouragement to an appeal to raise the necessary funding for this.

The church stands in a very fine churchyard with some fine monuments. The former Greater London Council recently provided new railings and base wall to match the design of the original, of which a few fragments remained.

St. Anne's Church, Limehouse

Detail of roof construction with new tubular steel trusses inserted within the existing roof space.

New Roof Trusses

All Saints Church, Poplar

All Saints is a very fine church of c1820 faced in Portland stone, designed by A W Hollis. It suffered damage during the war, but was later repaired. The Corporation has carried out the cleaning of the extension and a number of important repairs to the stonework and the roof, and the church itself has raised a considerable amount of money towards other works of repair.

The interior of All Saints was destroyed by a bomb during the war and the post-war rebuild left it without galleries. The organ was also destroyed. To replace it, a large Victorian organ was brought from a congregational church and was completely rebuilt with electric action by Noel Mander. This work was extremely well done and a fine instrument has been produced with a wide range of sounds for music from all periods.

The church stands in the middle of a large, well-kept churchyard with a number of table tombs, some of which are in need of repair. The landscaping also needs improvement to give a better setting for the church. The south part of the churchyard retains its original high quality cast-iron railings on a massive granite plinth.

All Saints Church, Poplar   Portico

St. Paul's Church, Shadwell

St. Paul's, Shadwell was built in 1818-21 to the design of John Walter on the site of an earlier church. It was one of the Waterloo Churches, built after Parliament had voted £1 million for the building of churches as a thank-offering for the nation's deliverance from conquest by Napoleon.

The original place of worship on the site was a chapel of ease, built in 1656 when Shadwell became the first of the Tower Hamlets to be separated from the great parish of Stepney. It was first rebuilt in 1669 – the last new church to be built in East London for 30 years.

During the 18th Century St. Paul's became known as 'the mariners' church'. Between 1725 and 1795 over 75 sea captains and their wives were buried in the churchyard. John Wesley preached there four times between 1770 and 1795 and gave his last recorded sermon in the church. Other famous names associated with the church include that of explorer Captain James Cook, the bans of whose marriage to Elizabeth Batts of Barking were called at St. Paul's and whose eldest son, James, was baptised there in 1763. St. Paul's is connected too with the American presidency: Jane Randolph, mother of Thomas Jefferson (the third President of the United States) was baptised there in 1718. Jane's parents' marriage was also celebrated in the church.

The church is of brick with stucco decoration, with a Gibbsian tower with circular upper stage. This has eight bells (not currently operative) and a good quality clock of the same date.

The interior, although small, is impressive. The shallow domed ceiling has a representation of the sun in the centre with a painted sky around it. Its organ is a particularly important discovery. Until a short time ago it was assumed that it was of the same date as the church, but research has shown that a substantial part dates from 1714 and is by Samuel Jordan, an important figure in the development of the English organ little of whose work survives. It is hoped that this organ, which has been broadcast on Radio 3, can be restored.

Repairs to the church and its surrounding walls and railings, and landscaping of the churchyard to provide public access to the north quay of Shadwell Basin, were carried out by the LDDC in 1983-84.

St. Peter's Church, Wapping

Designed by J F Pownall in 1866, St. Peter's was unfortunately never completed. Only the eastern half was built, and the church has no churchyard. It is nevertheless an important building of quality. Externally, the walls are of yellow brick with dark brick and stone decoration, obscured until recently by layers of dirt. The Corporation has helped to fund a cleaning programme, and the patterns are once again visible. The church itself has raised a considerable amount of money for re-roofing and other essential repairs, and for the provision of new heating equipment.

The church's interior is a splendid example of mid-Victorian polychromy, and its organ is a good quality Victorian instrument, rebuilt in the 1930s and converted to electric action.

St. Paul's Church, Shadwell

St. Peter's Church, Wapping

St. John's Church, Wapping

The former historic church of Wapping, St. John's was designed by Joel Johnson in 1756. Its tower, rising from the bombed ruins of the church, is now a prominent local landmark. The tower is in good condition, but of the remainder of the church only the vault and the north wall remain. A detailed study is needed to determine how the remains of the church might be treated, and as much of the ruins as possible retained.

St. John's historic churchyard, on the opposite side of Scandrett Street, is a pleasant small scale space protected by part of the great wall which surrounded the London Dock. The Corporation plans to carry out remedial landscaping having completed restoration work to the wall.

The Tower of St. John's Church, Wapping

St. Patrick's Church, Wapping

This Roman Catholic church lies immediately to the east of St. John's. It is a simple temple-like building of 1879, designed by E W Tasker and built from the 'penny a week' contributions from its mainly Irish congregation. It has a low pitched roof and overhanging eaves with stone bracketed cornice.

The church contains a magnificent Victorian marble altar. Its large simple space has a timber coffered barrel vault supported on tall Ionic columns. The chancel is defined by a change to the Corinthian order and a plaster vault.

The Corporation is to make a contribution towards cleaning and repair work.

The Altar of St. Patrick's Church, Wapping

St. Mary's Church, Rotherhithe

At the heart of the village of Rotherhithe was its parish church of St. Mary the Virgin: it is thought a church stood there in Saxon times. At one time the church was under the control of the great Benedictine Abbey of St. Saviour, Bermondsey: its first recorded rector was John de Toqueville, who was given the living by the Prior of Bermondsey in 1310. It was in this medieval church that the captain and the crew of the 'Mayflower' worshipped and in which her captain and part owner, Christopher Jones, was buried.

The church was rebuilt in 1715. The remains of the tower of the medieval church were incorporated within the brick-built 18th Century church, which has an octagonal obelisk spire and circular top stage of detached Corinthian columns. The interior still retains its 18th Century feel with a shallow vaulted ceiling and tall Ionic columns, though the galleries were removed by William Butterfield during his 'restoration' in 1876. At the east end is a fine 18th Century reredos, with panels painted in the 19th Century by Florence Nicholson. When the church was rebuilt Christopher Jones' grave disappeared along with many others, but the present church contains his monument, erected in 1965. Another fine monument in the church is that to Joseph Wade, King's Carver in His Majesty's Yards at Deptford and Woolwich, which has a Rococo cartouche. The organ of St. Mary's is an internationally known instrument of 1765 by Byfield which has been featured on several recordings. The organ case with its Doric entablature was erected in 1764.

The churchyard with its mature trees provides a charming setting for the church. Part, however, has been laid out as a playground, which is sadly not in keeping with the building.

Christ Church, Isle of Dogs

Christ Church is an imposing Victorian church of the 1880s designed by F Johnstone and built with funds provided by William Cubitt, the developer of Cubitt Town. It has a large spire which is a prominent local landmark and a good quality organ with pipe work thought to date back to the 17th Century. The organ has been extended over the years, culminating with a major rebuild in the 1950s by Noel Mander, and produces a superb sound that fills the church with its reverberent power. However, it now needs major attention and the LDDC is considering a grant for restoration and cleaning. The spire also needs structural repair and the LDDC is funding a study to establish its condition. Other work in which the Corporation has been involved includes the construction of community spaces within the church and proposed improvements to the landscape around it.

Christ Church, Isle of Dogs

St. Mary's Church, Rotherhithe

St. Paul's Presbyterian Church, Isle of Dogs

St. Paul's Presbyterian Church, Isle of Dogs

The foundation stone for this remarkable little chapel was laid in 1856 by John Scott Russell, the enterprising shipbuilder who was at this time building Brunel's 'Great Eastern Steamship' nearby. The church's architect was Thomas Knightley and the design, though small, uses an attractive combination of polychromatic brick and stone with Romanesque forms. An unusual feature of its construction is the cast-iron tracery of the windows, which it is possible were made in Scott Russell's shipyard. Strangely, in view of this, the construction of the lantern – which is such a feature of the design, is of timber. Another unusual feature is the laminated timber arches supporting the roof. Brunel was himself a pioneer of this form of construction and it is at least a possibility that the great engineer also had a hand in the design of the church.

The church has not been used as such for a number of years and, although used as a storage building, is badly in need of repair and regular maintenance. The architectural qualities of this delightful little building and its potential historic importance have, however, been recognised by the LDDC which has commissioned a survey of the building. It is hoped that a more suitable use can be found and restoration of this important, though little known, product of the Island's history carried out.

St. Mark's Church, Silvertown

An idiosyncratic building of polychromatic design in hollow ceramic blocks, brick and stone, this church was designed by S S Teulon, one of the masters of the style. The church became redundant and passed into the hands of the London Borough of Newham who intended it for use by the Passmore Edwards Museum. Before this could happen it was severely damaged by fire with the nave and chancel roofing destroyed and the interior stonework damaged.

Realising its national importance and its even greater local importance in an area of few important historic buildings, the Corporation has jointly sponsored the restoration of St. Mark's as a Museum of Victorian Life with the Passmore Edwards Trust. Finance has been made available by the Corporation and the London Borough of Newham to refurbish the building completely and to re-instate a replica of the original roof, re-using the original ironwork. The timber to be used for the roof trusses, very similar to the original timber, has been obtained from perfectly preserved piles removed from the river bed.

St. Mark's Church, Silvertown – Interior During Reconstruction

St. Mark's Church, Silvertown – After Fire

St. Olave's Church, Rotherhithe

The Norwegian Seamen's church in Lower Road, at the entry to Rotherhithe Tunnel, was designed in 1927 by John Seaton Dahl. It has overtones of the architecture of the Hanseatic ports, especially in its spire. The church appears to be in good condition, as does the more recent Finnish Seamen's church nearby in Albion Street, designed by Yorke Rosenberg and Mardall and very Scandinavian in appearance, with white walls and a slender grey slated campanile.

St. Olav's Church, Rotherhithe

St. James' Church, Bermondsey

Designed by James Savage and built in 1827-29, St. James' is one of the grandest of the so-called Waterloo Churches. It is sited on the LDDC boundary on the south side of Jamaica Road and, though not technically within Docklands, is very much part of Docklands' historic church heritage: its tower with its Baroque silhouette plays an important part in the Docklands urban environment. The west front has a powerful portico of unfluted Ionic columns. Internally the galleries, with their tall plain columns and Ionic capitals, remain. With the flat coffered ceiling they frame a projecting arched chancel containing a large painting of the Ascension of Christ by John Wood, painted in 1844.

Much of the church's stonework is now decaying and needs renewal, as do the slated roof and lead gutters; otherwise the church is in good structural condition but needs financial help as the small, but growing, congregation is unable to cope with the cost of repairs. To help answer these problems, the LDDC has suggested conversion to form a church at gallery level leaving a large space for other uses in the area currently occupied by the nave and aisles. (The aisles have already been enclosed beneath the galleries.) The fascinating crypt structure could also lend itself to conversion for other uses.

MARKS SILVERTOWN SOUTH ELEVATION CROSS SECTION

St. Mark's Church, Silvertown – Reconstruction Drawing

St. James' Church, Bermondsey

St. Matthias Church, Poplar

St. Matthias Church, Poplar – late 18th Century Watercolour

St. Matthias Church is the oldest known complete building in Docklands and as such is of the greatest historical importance. Built in 1654 as a chapel for the East India Company (the organisation that was responsible for much of the early economic activity of the area), it was constructed of brick with stone dressings and internally was a most advanced piece of architecture for its date. In plan, it is of a cross form with aisles, with the roof supported on huge oak columns, one of which was replaced by stone, probably in the 18th Century.

The building became a church in 1866 and the exterior was subsequently encased in Kentish ragstone and given a decidedly eccentric, medieval appearance by W W Teulon, brother of S S Teulon, the architect of St. Mark's, Silvertown. The original base to the cupola was encased by a larger and flimsy turret and a chancel was added at the east end.

The building ceased to be used as a church about eight years ago, and an outbreak of dry rot, following theft of lead from the roofs, led to much of the interior being gutted. Nevertheless, even in its present decayed state, the interior is a magnificent space. The LDDC is anxious that this important building should be brought back into public use, and has promoted a scheme for its adaptation into a centre for the performing arts, with special emphasis on small scale performances of Baroque music which would be particularly relevant to this English Baroque building. Indeed the restoration of this originally Baroque chapel and its conversion for use for the performance of Baroque music would be a major artistic and cultural achievement.

To this end the Corporation is setting up a Trust with the Raglan Baroque Players (whose sponsor is Lord Raglan), a young orchestra with a growing international reputation, and is embarking on extensive restoration work to return the exterior to its original appearance by removing the cladding and returning the windows and door openings to their original design. The original eaves brackets all survive so the extent of original walls is clearly defined, and where the stone cladding has come away the brickwork underneath appears to be in good condition. The interior is still very much in its original form but the present medieval style windows are quite out of character: replacement windows of the original type would have a beneficial architectural effect. The internal walls carry many fine monuments to famous local people and to servants of the East India Company. One – a monument by Flaxman – has been removed for safe-keeping, but ought to be returned once the church is restored.

The church is set in what was once a country churchyard, and even now retains a country churchyard atmosphere. Gravestones and tombs should be left in their existing locations wherever possible, if this atmosphere is not to be destroyed.

St. Matthias Church, Poplar, 1986

Interior of Church, 1986

Ceiling Boss

St. Matthias Church, Poplar showing possible use for performances of Baroque opera

HMS 'Belfast' and Jetty

New Jetty at Thames Tunnel Mills

Dock and Riverside Structures

The river is the very heart of Docklands and its dock structures – though very different in character from its churches and public buildings – sometimes also exhibit a monumental form. This is true especially of the dock boundary walls. The most dramatic of the river structures are, however, the locks and lock gates: when the locks are emptied for repair to their walls or gates, these immense structures are revealed in all their Piranesian grandeur.

Careful conservation of the riverside is important. It forms the setting for very many of Docklands' new developments, and if existing riverside features were lost or ignored, the shoreline would lose much of its interest and variety.

River Walls and Jetties

Development along the river-bank has always been carried out in a piecemeal way. Ideally a river-wall – or bank – was established to keep the river from overflowing onto the surrounding marshland. This has been done in many places, giving rise to such names as Wapping Wall and Millwall (named after the windmills along the river-bank). As the riverside was developed, owners would build out into the river to form wharves on which their buildings would stand. This encroachment progressed further out into the river as buildings became larger.

This pattern of development has given much of the river-bank an interesting modelled plan form, with some wharves set forward from others, in many cases with small scale inlets between them, adjacent wharves often standing at slightly different angles to each other. These subtle variations can easily be lost when large scale riverside wall works are carried out, the new wall typically following a straight line. Even when variations in plan are introduced, the result may still often be dull if the same materials are used throughout.

Many wharves had jetties in front of them. These were usually constructed of timber, although there were some built of iron or concrete. Today, jetties can be brought back into use very effectively as features in riverside walks. A good example of a form of jetty construction suitable for use in conjunction with historic warehouses (and reminiscent of the jetties in paintings of Gravesend a hundred years ago by Tissot) may be seen at New Concordia Wharf, where the jetty is built of massive greenhart piles with timber decking; another is at Thames Tunnel Mills.

Stairs

Access to the river by watermen and their passengers was by a series of stairs which led down to stone-built hards built out to the low-watermark. These stairs were approached by narrow passages running between the towering warehouses or often through tunnels in the warehouses themselves. Good examples of the latter can be seen at the former Courage's Horselydown Brewery and at Reeds Wharf, Bermondsey, where the opening to the river is at the end of Mill Street, the approach tunnel running under the building and forming an extension to the street itself.

Many of the stairs were unfortunately closed in the 1930s for safety reasons (local children used the stairs to swim out to the lighters moored in the river) although they remained legal right of way, keys to the passages being available on request. This was clearly not a convenient arrangement, and the stairs consequently became disused and gradually fell into disrepair. More recently, many of the river stairs have been listed because of their historical importance. The LDDC would like to see these historic accesses to the river brought back into use, and proposes to carry out a feasibility study to see if this can be achieved.

Draw Docks

Another form of historic access to the river is the draw dock, effectively a narrow sloping beach on which barges were allowed to dry out at low water when they would be unloaded. Examples in Docklands include the Newcastle Draw Dock. At present rather derelict, there are plans to remove rubbish and replace the mud on the bottom with a sloping ground beach at an angle that will make it 'self-cleaning.' With other landscape improvements Newcastle Draw Dock could become an attractive and interesting place for visitors. Another is Johnson's Draw Dock, at the bottom of the Isle of Dogs. This had been taken over by a scrap metal merchant and closed off to the public: the Corporation would like to see it restored as a public access to the river.

Dock Retaining Walls

The dock walls supporting the quays and containing the water basins are nowadays recognised for the important engineering structures that they are. Some sections of dock retaining wall are indeed considered of such importance that they are listed Grade I. The engineering and workmanship in these structures is usually of the highest quality, especially in the earlier docks, and the Corporation attaches great importance to their conservation.

Prior to the establishment of the LDDC, many dock walls were lost when the docks were indiscriminately filled. At London Dock's in Wapping the original dock walls survived this policy, and the LDDC has now ensured their preservation by using them as enclosing walls to part of a new amenity canal, designed and built by the LDDC. The engineering of the original part of the London Dock's must be considered the best in the Port of London. Exposed in all their grandeur by the change of levels, Rennie's dock walls with their stone binding courses are now clearly displayed.

At the St. Katharine Docks the structure of the docks themselves is more or less unaltered, even though most of the splendid Telford warehouses have been demolished. The Royal Victoria, Royal Albert and King George V Docks in Newham have been acquired by the Corporation

and are awaiting redevelopment. Surviving artefacts within the dock's have been identified and whoever carries out the redevelopment of these docks will be encouraged to conserve them.

Docks and Dry Docks

In the Surrey Docks, the listed original brick dock walls of the 1890s at Greenland Dock have been repaired. The entrance lock is no longer in use and a dam carrying a road has been built across it. Nevertheless the lock, also listed, is being restored, the lock operating machinery (originally under steel covers) has been exposed and restored and the whole area has been laid out so that the operation of the lock may be readily understood.

The South Dock is faced in superb quality ashlar stonework, generally in good condition, which has been cleaned of oil stains and repaired. The listed entrance has been fitted with modern gates matching the old gates, and is to be re-opened. Bollards, capstans and other artefacts are being restored around the dock. It is the intention that each part of the restored dock will add extra interest to the surrounding new developments.

The East India Docks in Poplar are now owned by the LDDC. The East India Import Dock was drained during the war to enable Mulberry harbour units to be constructed within it. The dock walls collapsed, and it has since mostly been filled. The entrance basin remains, however, and it is intended to retain this together with the now listed entrance lock, and conserve them in an interpretive way as at Greenland Dock. Similarly, the Grade I listed walls of the West India Export Docks in the Isle of Dogs are being carefully protected in the detailed design of new buildings on West Quay and Heron Quays.

Apart from some later dry docks accessible from the docks themselves there are only two surviving sites with dry docks on the riverside in Docklands: Blackwall Yard, Poplar and Nelson Dock in Southwark. The Blackwall Yard has two dry docks, one of which is still operational:

Western Dock, London Docks

Greenland Dock

Bridge over South Lock, Surrey Docks before Restoration

23

Greenland Lock

Bridge over Shadwell Basin Entrance Lock, London Docks

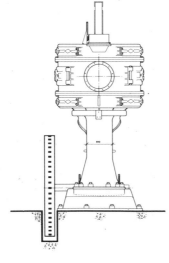

This large vacuum pump was used in the operation of pneumatic grain elevators which discharged grain from ships at the Rank Hovis McDougall Flour mill in the Royal Victoria Dock.

the site has been acquired for redevelopment and this use will soon cease. The second is listed, and although it is in very poor condition the developer is considering restoring it. The small dry dock at Nelson Dock is unfortunately also in poor condition and its restoration as a working dry dock is now inconceivable. This site has also been acquired for redevelopment, but it is hoped that the developers will be able to retain the form of the dock in some way when redevelopment work is carried out. Of particular interest here is the unusually shaped iron caisson which ought to be retained in situ, even if it is filled behind with concrete to form a new river wall.

This same policy of restoring and displaying surviving dock structures and equipment of historical interest will be carried out, where appropriate, on other sites owned by the Corporation. Where docks are in other ownerships, owners will be encouraged to respect their historic character and restore their equipment.

Bridges, Cranes and Machinery

Apart from the dock structures themselves, Docklands boasts a number of bridges of historic interest, and cranes, pumps and other pieces of dock equipment have been uncovered in the process of restoration work. Wherever possible such features are being restored and displayed as a reminder of the area's industrial past.

Three characteristic iron swing footbridges of historic interest are to be seen at Greenland/South Dock. The footbridge over the Greenland Dock is of an attractive arched lattice design, hydraulically operated. A second, over the Steelyard Cut (between Greenland and South Docks) is too small for general service use by the public but has nevertheless been restored. The South Dock bridge has had its turning gear destroyed and embedded in concrete. As the lock is to be made operational, the bridge is to be moved to another location within Greenland Dock over the former Norway cutting, where it will be restored to its original appearance using the original engineer's working

drawings recently discovered by the LDDC.

Other historic bridges in the area include those at Shadwell Basin (part of the London Docks, Wapping). Here two extremely interesting steel bascule bridges have been restored as static bridges at Glamis Road and Garnet Street. A similar type of bridge is also being restored across the lock entry to Surrey Water at Rotherhithe, whilst one of a pair of swing bridges over the entry to London Dock from Tobacco Dock has been restored in its present location connecting East Quay pedestrian route with Tobacco Dock and the Skin Floor.

For many years the skyline of Docklands was dominated by its huge dock cranes. The cranes at the West India, Millwall and Royal Victoria Docks have been retained with dramatic effect. Other items of machinery are also discovered from time to time: where possible they are being used in the redevelopment of the area as features of historic and landscape interest. For example, a large vacuum pump used for grain handling at the Royal Victoria Dock, which the Corporation has had dismantled and restored, is to be mounted on a plinth close to the housing development by Roger Malcolm Limited in the south-east corner of Millwall Dock, the place where this type of equipment was first pioneered. The machine looks like a large steam engine and has an impressive sense of scale, standing about four metres high on its plinth.

Not only does the displaying of artefacts at strategic locations provide links with the past, it also adds considerable interest to the many walks in the area; for this reason, conservation and display are encouraged on private development sites as well as on Corporation-owned land.

To date the LDDC has stored a number of artefacts found within the docks. Among these are pumps from the pump house at the London Dock, bollards and a cannon, all of which the Corporation intends to restore and mount in suitable locations. A number of cast-iron columns have been similarly preserved and will be incorporated into new buildings and landscaping.

Cranes in the West India Docks

The Warehouses

The building type most readily associated with Docklands, the warehouses stand very much as a feature on their own, and have contributed greatly to the atmosphere of the dock and riverside areas. A number of those that remain are listed Grade I, a category of listing which is only applied to the most important of historic buildings. The earliest surviving warehouses in Docklands are granaries in Rotherhithe dating from the 1790s. The small granary adjacent to The Mayflower public house was restored at an early date and is one of the earliest examples of successful conservation of this building type. There are other granaries on the south side of the river, recognisable by their small openings with inward-opening windowless timber shutters. Generally, the floor to ceiling heights in such buildings were fairly low, and successful conservation demands imaginative schemes for adaptations to make the maximum use of existing internal structures.

The Skin Floor

The new docks built at the beginning of the 19th Century were equipped with large, new, bonded warehouses. The most intensive developments of these splendid buildings were at the London and St. Katharine Docks, though sadly most have now been demolished. However at the London Dock there survives a unique building called the Skin Floor (the name comes from its use as a store for imported furs), built in 1811-18 to the design of D A Alexander as a tobacco warehouse. It is now listed Grade I. Over the years, parts of the Skin Floor have been demolished but a substantial amount still remains. The structure comprises a series of parallel roofs with timber trusses, with canted queen posts surmounted by long lantern lights. The roofs are supported on a system of cast-iron columns which branch out, giving the appearance of trees in a forest when viewed obliquely. Beneath this is a large area of former wine vaults. Vaults such as these once extended under most of the

The Skin Floor

Tree-like Columns in the Skin Floor

quays of the London and St. Katharine Docks and those of the Skin Floor are almost the only surviving examples.

The Skin Floor was empty and derelict for many years but Tobacco Dock Development Limited has now begun an exciting and sensitive conservation scheme in which the structure will be completely restored and adapted to provide shopping and restaurants, which it is hoped will attract a large number of visitors and create many new permanent jobs in the area. The scheme has attracted an urban development grant from the London Borough of Tower Hamlets, and the LDDC has been sufficiently encouraged by the quality of the work proposed to enable the scheme to go ahead by providing generous financial assistance towards repairs in the form of an historic buildings grant.

The West India Dock Sugar Warehouses

The other particularly important warehouse structures within Docklands are two large early 19th Century sugar warehouses in the West India Docks. One of the two was originally one of six large warehouses built for the opening of the docks in 1802. The last surviving multi-storey dock warehouses of the late Georgian period in London, both are listed Grade I.

The Corporation, which at present owns the warehouses, is in the course of appointing a developer to adapt these buildings and those adjacent, to form part of an exciting new leisure complex. Fundamental to the scheme is the need to respect the warehouses' historic character and retain as much as possible of their existing structure; it has been agreed that new structures will be sensitively inserted into the present structures with their timber and cast-iron columns and massive timber floors, to ensure maximum expression of the buildings' existing features. The complex is expected to become a major tourist facility, to be known as Port East.

Vaults under the Skin Floor, Tobacco Dock

Sugar Warehouse One, West India Import Dock

Cast-iron Window, Warehouse One

Sugar Warehouse Two, West India Import Dock

Olivers Wharf

New Concordia Wharf

New Concordia Wharf

Olivers Wharf and New Concordia Wharf

The other category of warehouse in Docklands is the large and imposing Victorian riverside warehouse. Such warehouses were built in large numbers after the Customs Consolidation Act of 1853 allowed their use as bonded stores. The first of these in Docklands to be converted into housing was Olivers Wharf in Wapping which, unusually for a warehouse, was in the Victorian Gothic tradition, rather than the more usual 'Engineers Classical' derived style. Another, excellent example of how a warehouse type building can be successfully adapted to a new use can be seen at the New Concordia Wharf housing development at St. Saviour's Dock, Bermondsey. Great attention has been paid to detail here, each part of the design being in sympathy with the original.

The iron columns have been coated with intumescent mastic as a fire protection and the timber floor structure has been retained, although – for necessary fire protection – a concrete slab has been laid on top, ensuring that there would be no collapse even if the joists were burnt away beneath it. (The loss of the original timber floorboarding is not considered too important: large areas will be covered with carpets and furniture and much of the floor area will not be visible.) The large timber beams are of sufficient section to be protected by their own charring. Visually, the timber joisted ceilings, which have now been cleaned, provide a most attractive feature.

The wall cranes on the dockside at New Concordia were restored with the aid of an Historic Buildings Council grant: although they are electric cranes dating only from the 1930s they add a powerful vertical element to the building which enlivens its façades. The new jetty has been constructed in the same way as was done in the 19th Century using massive greenhart piles and timber decking.

New Concordia Wharf

The Butler's Wharf Group

Up river from New Concordia Wharf is the huge complex of warehouses of the Butler's Wharf group. The most dramatic part of the complex is the section along Shad Thames: here the tall warehouse buildings rise sheer from the backline of the pavements on both sides of the street which is crossed by bridges at all levels, giving perhaps the closest approximation to Piranesi's 'Carceri' ever produced in a built form.

The original Butler's Wharf building, now listed Grade II, is located immediately downstream from the former Courage's Horselydown Brewery: it features prominently in the view from Tower Bridge and the St. Katharine Docks. Butler's Wharf had suffered badly over the years as a result of alterations carried out to enable more modern cranes to be installed. Windows had been filled, cornices removed and concrete platforms built out. On top of this, half the eastern wing was demolished following a fire, with the result that the original form of the building was until recently almost entirely indiscernible. A photograph taken from Tower Bridge during its construction fortunately shows Butler's Wharf in its full Victorian splendour. From this, and from measurements taken on site, the LDDC was able to commission a reconstruction drawing (undertaken by Donald Insall, the

drawing was subsequently displayed in the 1984 Royal Academy Summer Exhibition) and has been able to use its influence as planning authority to require a unified scheme of restoration based on the reconstruction drawing, to be carried out jointly by Messrs Clarke London Limited and Conran Roche, developers of the western and eastern wings. The first part of the work has now been completed. The Corporation has paid great attention to faithful reproduction of the architectural details in granting listed building consent. This will be carried through into the larger second stage, to be undertaken by Butler's Wharf Limited.

Butler's Wharf, c1890

Shad Thames

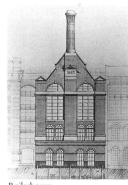

Boilerhouse

Butler's Wharf, c1983

ER'S WHARF REDEVELOPMENT

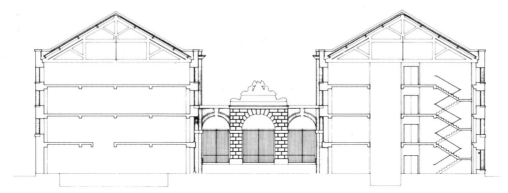

Free Trade Wharf, cross section.

Free Trade Wharf longitudinal section showing restored colonnade.

Gun Wharf

Free Trade Wharf, Shadwell

Free Trade Wharf, Shadwell is a large warehouse built by the East India Company in the 1870s to the designs of Richard Jupp. Unfortunately, it was very insensitively altered in the 1930s with concrete floors inserted, the courtyard built over and additions built on to the river end, and until recently has presented a very dilapidated appearance. The present developers, Regalian Limited, have been encouraged and assisted with professional advice by the LDDC to carry out sensitive conservation work. The courtyard is being opened up and later additions removed. The original entrance gateway, of which only the coat of arms now remains, will be restored. It is unfortunately not possible to remove the concrete floors within the building and, as these do not relate to the original window levels, a new arrangement of window openings has had to be devised: the splendid arcade at the lower levels will, however, be retained. There is no doubt that the work being carried out at Free Trade Wharf will bring about a dramatic transformation of this building, demonstrating how much can be achieved by skilful conservation.

Warehouse Conversions

One of the most successful of the warehouse housing conversions carried out in Docklands is that by the London & Quadrant Housing Association of Thames Tunnel Mills, a former flour mill, assisted by a grant from the Historic Buildings Council for England before it was absorbed within the Historic Buildings and Monuments Commission, English Heritage.

These warehouse conversions are providing a rather special, exciting form of housing which is bringing large numbers of people to live in Docklands, and have encouraged the development of surrounding sites for housing of a quality that might not otherwise have been possible. It is likely that this will lead in time to the development of community services and facilities too.

The viability of such warehouse conversions in Docklands has been amply demonstrated over the past few years by small entreprencurial developers with vision. As a result, the larger national developers have now become interested and are themselves carrying out warehouse adaptations, primarily for housing. An excellent scheme of refurbishment containing an arcaded public river walk has, for example, been carried out at Gun Wharf in Wapping by Barratt (East London) Limited.

Developers were initially interested only in buildings with river views. Warehouse conversions have generally proved so successful, however, that schemes are now being carried out on warehouses located away from the river – a particularly pleasing development, and one very much in line with the LDDC's conservation policies. Strict rules, however, govern the granting of building consent to convert listed warehouses to new uses. Such buildings were originally listed as warehouses, and their historic character and form derive from that use. The Corporation therefore tries to ensure that any alterations are such that this character is not lost: the reason for their listing would otherwise cease to exist. This means that the retention of the original windows, doors and frames is to be a pre-condition of listed building consent. Where new windows or doors are required for practical reasons, they must be of a design that reflects the original. Similarly, new features such as balconies must be sympathetically designed. In some cases it has been felt necessary to gut out the existing structure for redevelopment purposes: this is only accepted by the LDDC where no alternative to complete demolition exists. As the designers of New Concordia Wharf have shown, it may often be possible to retain both the existing structure and interior of a listed warehouse with considerable success.

The Corporation is also concerned to ensure that as many as possible of the surviving historic artefacts relating to the former use of warehouses are retained. The iron wall cranes, for example, should be left in their original

Thames Tunnel Mills

New Concordia Wharf

Thames Tunnel Mills

'New Concordia', modern flat in the new penthouse

New Concordia Wharf, open timber roof.

Hay's Galleria, interior under construction

Hay's Galleria, seen from Custom House Quay

Hay's Galleria as proposed in 1982, drawn by Albert Timothy

locations. Similarly, the original hydraulic 'jiggers,' which rise through several floors, may still exist and if moved to a public multi-storey space such as a staircase or a courtyard, can be excitingly displayed.

The most dramatic conversion of former warehouses in Docklands is undoubtedly that of Hays Dock, Bermondsey, carried out by the St. Martins Property Corporation, where a new tourist attraction in the form of a glazed 'Galleria' with shops, bars and restaurants forms the space between the original warehouse blocks. Another sensitively executed conversion is the adaptation of adjacent Chamberlains Wharf to a private hospital. If the approach adopted in these and other successful developments can be maintained, warehouses converted to new uses will retain as much of their original character as possible, so that future generations will be able to understand their history.

Industrial Buildings

There are relatively few surviving historic industrial buildings in Docklands compared with the much larger number of warehouses. There are, however, examples of a particularly interesting building type – the hydraulic pumping station.

Hydraulic power came into widespread use in the second half of the 19th Century. The London Hydraulic Pumping Company (LHP) obtained an Act of Parliament to construct a series of pumping stations in London in 1884 and a network of mains supplying hydraulic power to operate lifts and machinery was constructed over a wide area of the capital. There are two hydraulic pumping stations in Docklands – at Rotherhithe and at Shadwell Basin in Wapping, the Wapping station being the last to supply hydraulic power as a public utility.

At Wapping, because the public was being supplied, the water was filtered. It was pumped from the dock or artesian well into the tanks on the roof, from where it was fed by gravity into large underground cisterns: from these the water was pumped by steam engines into the mains. The function of the accumulator tower, which is the station's most striking architectural feature, was to provide a reservoir of water at constant pressure in the mains and to act as a control device for the steam engines. Although the designer of the building is not known, the machinery for this and other LHP stations was supplied by the Hydraulic Engineering Company of Chester whose engineer was E B Ellington, an energetic advocate of public utility hydraulic power stations.

The Shadwell building is not in the architectural tradition of London's industrial buildings; with its hard looking and evenly coloured dark red brick and brown Mansfield stone, it is much more reminiscent of such buildings in the north-west, which suggests it may have been designed by an engineer from the Chester company. The station's original Fairbairn-Beeley boilers were later replaced by Babcock and Wilcox boilers. Because of their

great height, this necessitated the raising of the two middle tanks in a crude adaptation above the boiler house. A new engine house containing steam driven pumps was built into the south side of the engine house in the 1920s and the steam pumps were taken out in the 1950s and replaced by electrically driven pumps.

Because it is among the last hydraulic power stations remaining in Britain Shadwell has been given the high Grade II* listing by the Department of the Environment. It ceased pumping in 1977 and is now owned by the LDDC. Proposals to adapt the building as a recording studio and rehearsal room for the orchestra of the Academy of St. Martin-in-the-Fields are well advanced, and a joint company of the LDDC and the Academy will carry out the refurbishment and adaptation of the building for its new use: plans include a restaurant looking across Shadwell Basin and a viewing gallery for the public.

Wapping Hydraulic Pumping Station

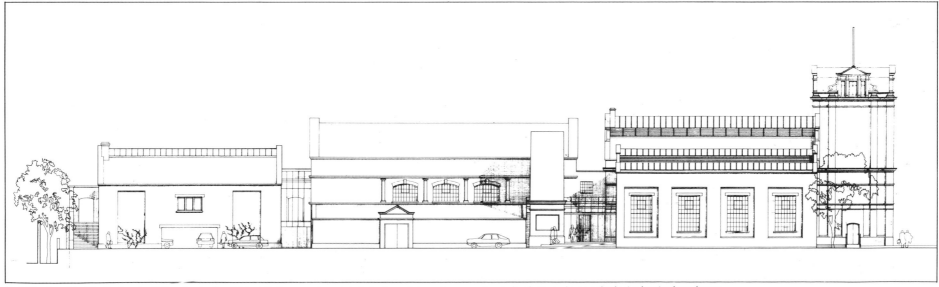

South Elevation of the Wapping Pumping Station, showing from left to right, the new restaurant, the boiler house, to be used as a recording studio, the Engine house, to be the Academy's rehearsal room, and finally the accumulator tower.

Shipyards

Shipbuilding and shiprepair are among the oldest of the industries of London. The Thames was formerly the largest and most technologically advanced centre of shipbuilding in the world. Not only were the most advanced ships built in yards along the stretch of the river which passes through Docklands (ships like HMS 'Warrior', the first ironclad ship), but it was here also that some of the most important marine engine builders of the 19th Century were located. Sadly, few industrial buildings or structures of historic or architectural interest from this era survive. Of those that do, the Nelson Dockyard and Burrell's Wharf are the most interesting and important.

The Nelson Dockyard, to the north of Greenland Dock in the Surrey Docks peninsula, was used for shipbuilding from the 17th Century until about 1870 when it became used solely for shiprepair until its closure in 1968. The yard was the home of many important shipbuilders, among them John Taylor, Randall and Brent, and Thomas Bilbe. John Taylor built the 50-gun warship 'Portland' there in 1652 and a further seven warships between then and 1702. The families of Randall and Brent operated the yard after 1745 and under various partnerships it became the greatest rival to the Blackwall Yard, said to be the largest private dockyard in the world in the 18th Century. Randall and Brent are credited with having built at least two hundred ships at the Nelson Dockyard, among them thirty warships and at least one East Indiaman a year between 1756 and 1813.

The firm of S D Brent, which managed the yard after Randall and Brent, were among the earliest builders of steamships: they built one of the first steamships, the 'Diana', in 1917. But it was Thomas Bilbe and Co. who developed some of the most advanced methods of construction. Bilbe's were builders of fast sailing ships for the China trade and Thomas Bilbe's first ships were of timber using radiating diagonal framing to give longitudinal strength. In 1856, however, Bilbe devised his own system of composite shipbuilding using timber planking fixed to iron frames. The lightness and strength of the structure were combined with a timber covering that could be sheathed in copper below water level, thus inhibiting the build-up of barnacles that would slow the ship down. The 'Red Riding Hood', considered to be the first composite construction tea clipper, was built by Bilbe in 1857. These light and incredibly fast vessels, of which the 'Cutty Sark' preserved in dry dock at Greenwich (though built on the Clyde) is the most famous, were particularly suited to the China trade.

The most important building and structures still in existence at the Nelson Dockyard today are the dry dock (probably built in 1790), the slipways (probably dating from c1645 when Rogue's map shows a large inlet, presumably one of Taylor's slips) and the 'Patent Slip' which extended 149 feet into the river: it was installed by Thomas Bilbe in 1855. A 'patent slip' has a carriage on which a ship is hauled out of the water for repair: the building housing the machinery for hauling the carriage out of the water (which appears on the 1868 ordnance survey) is in two parts, gable-ended onto Rotherhithe Street, with the machinery between. Although the present machinery dates from about 1900 it is still intact, and is one of the best surviving pieces of hydraulic machinery in Docklands.

It is, however, the splendid Grade II* Nelson House which is the most attractive architectural feature of the yard with its delightful octagonal cupola providing views of the river. Probably dating from about 1850, the house would have been built for one of the shipbuilding owners – perhaps Thomas Bilbe. Its function was clearly related to the shipyard; the grand Doric doorcase in the rear elevation provides direct access to the yard.

The second group of industrial listed buildings of great interest are those of Burrell's Wharf at the southern end of the Isle of Dogs, which incorporates many buildings of the famous Scott Russell shipbuilding yard. It was here in the years 1853 to 1858 that Scott Russell built the 'Great

Nelson House, Rotherhithe Street

Eastern Steamship,' an epic struggle that brought about his bankruptcy and the early death of her designer Isambard Kingdom Brunel, probably the most heroic figure of all 19th Century engineers. The construction of the 'Great Eastern' was undoubtedly the single most important event in the history of the Isle of Dogs and one which, for its time, was recorded by an unprecedented number of photographs.

Burrell's Wharf, once known as the Millwall Ironworks, was first laid out as a shipbuilding yard by William Fairbairn, a pioneer of structural ironwork. It was here that structural models of Stephenson's Brittania Bridge were built and tested. Fairbairn's main works were in Manchester, but the shipyard he set up in Millwall in 1836 was the first site in England to be laid out specifically for shipbuilding. The yard was purchased in 1847 by three

brothers – Henry, Richard and Alfred Robinson, and it was they who invited John Scott Russell to join them in a new shipbuilding venture. It is not known when the present buildings were built but parts of them appear in the background of contemporary photographs of the building of the 'Great Eastern' between 1853 and 1858.

The 'Great Eastern Steamship'

THE "GREAT EASTERN" STEAM-SHIP BUILDING ON THE STOCKS, MILLWALL, 22,500 TONS BURDEN.—FROM A PHOTOGRAPH IN THE POSSESSION OF MR. SCOTT RUSSELL.

The main building is of great interest. The roof has large queen-post trusses, the timbers of which are in pairs, joined by cast-iron junction pieces. These have the name 'William Cubitt' cast into them. As he was one of the largest contractors in London at the time, as well as having sizeable local interests, it is almost certain that he was the builder and probably the designer. The bottom members of the trusses support the large timber floor of the 'Mold' loft on which the lines of the frames of the 'Great Eastern' would have been set out.

Below the 'Mold' floor the building comprised a large open space with a gallery down one side. The gallery was supported by very heavy cast-iron 'I' section stanchions with open webs, fitted to take line shafting to drive the machines. A wooden pattern for one of these still survives in the roof space. The space below was probably taken up with workshops.

On the south end of the building is a tower which contained a large water tank to provide a ready supply in case of fire (though ironically, it could not be used when fire devasted the yard in 1853), and next to it the staircase topped with a bell turret which can just be seen above the great ship in its cradle in a number of contemporary photographs.

Other original buildings within the Burrell's Wharf complex are the office buildings adjacent to West Ferry Road. A few years ago three models of ships were found in the attic of one of these – a historic reminder of its former use. The large chimney of a particularly distinguished design, unfortunately truncated a number of years ago, was also part of the original complex. The base is octagonal and has a blank arcade, the arches of which are formed in bricks with large projecting keystones. This feature may well be a Cubitt motif: it can also be seen in the arches of the main building, as well as in a building facing the site across the road and it also occurs on a cottage next to The Lord Nelson public house in Manchester Road.

A further reminder of the 'Great Eastern Steamship' was brought to light in 1983 when, during the reclamation of the adjacent Napier Yard by the LDDC, part of the massive slipway on which the great ship was launched was discovered. This comprised large horizontal timbers parallel to the river fixed to timber piles. The timber slips, where they had been surrounded by clay, were in perfect condition apart from a little degradation of the surface, and when core samples were taken, the timber smelt as if it had been freshly sawn. The piles have been preserved in situ. The horizontal timbers are drying out prior to preservation treatment for ultimate public display.

Facing Burrell's Wharf across West Ferry Road is another building of the former shipyard complex. On the wall of this is a cast-iron plate with the monogram 'CJM & Co. 1860'. These are the initials of C J Mare, a pioneer iron shipbuilder, who took over the site after the demise of Scott Russell.

Public Buildings

Public buildings within Docklands are not of a monumental type, most having been built to house the expansion of public services following the legislative reforms of the late 19th Century. However, there are a number of town halls, schools, libraries and police and fire stations of note.

The former Poplar Town Hall building in Poplar High Street is listed Grade II. A high Victorian building in a free Gothic Style, it is well detailed throughout. It has recently been brought back into use as a local housing office by Tower Hamlets Council. A grant from the LDDC has enabled the exterior to be cleaned, and missing features restored. The cleaning has revealed the polychromy of the brickwork and the interesting carving can now be appreciated.

Another former town hall building within the LDDC area is that at Limehouse. Also listed Grade II, this was built in 1879 in white brick with white stone dressings in a Victorian form of the classical style. The arched entrance is set between two pairs of polished granite columns with

Poplar Town Hall

Corinthian capitals supporting a simple entablature. Above is a shallow projecting bay surmounted by a small pediment with a carved tympanum. The building is currently used by the National Museum of Labour History.

A short distance along Commercial Road is the former Passmore Edwards Library (now the Limehouse District Library), listed Grade II. It was built in 1900 with Messrs Clarkson as architects. At ground floor level it is of rusticated white stone with vermiculated quoins, while the difference in the design of the projecting wings shows the typically Victorian approach to design of setting up an axis of symmetry only to nullify it by a minor deviation on one side. The first floor is of white stone in the centre with two projecting wings of yellow brick enlivened with white stone pilasters on the corners, the entablatures of which support Flemish gables. The front area is surrounded by attractive Art Nouveau railings.

There are two other good library buildings in the Isle of Dogs, one being the Carnegie Public Library in Strattondale Street (a handsome Edwardian stone building of 1904 with a timber cupola), the other the former Poplar Library in the High Street. Adjacent to this is the former Poplar Technical College. Among the skills taught here in the heyday of the Port of London were navigation and marine engineering. One of the remarkable buildings designed by the LCC Architects Department under W E Riley, the college was built in 1906. Although based on classical idioms, the street frontage is a powerful free-style design executed in Portland stone. The entrance, with its carved stone surround, is at the extreme right, while at first floor level is a colonnade set asymmetrically within the facade. Doric columns are set in pairs with round-headed windows between. In order to emphasise the freeness of the design, a similar window is set immediately to the left of the colonnade.

In addition a number of large school buildings of considerable architectural merit survive within Docklands, most of them built around the turn of the century by the London School Board under E R Robson. These so-called 'towers of learning' are large buildings, designed to rise above the surrounding houses. Their effect upon the Docklands landscape must have been even more dramatic before the high-rise developments of the 1960s. An example of this type of building is the Harbinger Road Primary School, Isle of Dogs, an attractive red brick Gothic style building of 1908.

Poplar Technical College

37

Former St. Olave's Grammar School

18th Century Schoolhouse, St. Mary's, Rotherhithe

However, a really splendid example of a school building of this period is the South London College in Tooley Street, Bermondsey. Now listed Grade II, the school was built in 1893 for the long established St. Olave's Grammar School. E W Mountford's design is a mixture of late 19th Century Baroque and Arts and Crafts free-style, executed in red brick and white stone. It displays the high level of craftsmanship achieved by the end of the century, with great care and consideration given to every detail and each material used. Even now, after ninety years of pollution, the detail remains in good condition and the whole area has benefited enormously from the recent cleaning of the building.

Docklands also has three 18th Century charity school buildings, all of which are of great architectural interest. One of the three is at Rotherhithe; the other two – the Scandrett Street and Raine Street schools – are in Wapping. The privately owned Scandrett Street School is vacant, partially derelict, and in need of extensive repair. That at Raine Street, however, is currently being extended by English Heritage Architects as agents for the London Borough of Tower Hamlets.

The final group of buildings of note in the Docklands area are its fire and police stations. Millwall Fire Station at the south end of the Isle of Dogs, is an attractive Queen Anne style fire station built in 1904. Another example of the high standard of design achieved by the LCC Architects Department at this period, it is of brick with shallow brick pilasters, above a rendered base. The centre pilasters are set further apart and support a broken pediment. Fire stations were residential buildings at that time and in the rear yard is a small terrace of fire officers' cottages. The station is not listed by the Department of the Environment but is a good example of the kind of building which would appear on the LDDC's local list, with a recommendation that consideration be given to official listing.

Another fire station building of interest in Docklands, although in this instance now in another use, is that in Tooley Street, Bermondsey. This is a large, red brick Victorian Gothic building of c1870 with steeply pitched roofs and prominent chimneys. At ground floor level the two arches for the horse-drawn fire engines can still be seen.

At Wapping is the river police station for Docklands, now listed Grade II. This was built in 1907-10 and was designed by J D Butler, the Metropolitan Police Architect, in a Norman Shaw derived style. It is constructed of brown bricks with Portland stone dressings. The river elevation has, within a rectangular façade, a powerful stone gable projecting forward from the plane of the wall. Under this are two rows of projecting bay windows, that on the right starting above a large opening to the former boat house.

A former river police station in Coldharbour, Isle of Dogs, designed by the same architect's father, is also listed Grade II.

Public Houses

Docklands' riverside pubs have been well known to the general public since the last century, when engravings of The Grapes at Limehouse were published. Many are now listed buildings.

The Grapes is the archetypal riverside pub, built off the quay wall with a timber balcony projecting over the water. It features in Dickens' 'Our Mutual Friend' as 'The Six Jolly Fellowship Porters.' Perhaps better known is The Prospect of Whitby at Wapping, another fine example, as are The Angel and Mayflower in Rotherhithe. These pubs, while retaining their external appearance, have been much changed over the years by alterations.

Also in Wapping is The Town of Ramsgate, now dwarfed by the adjacent warehouse – a juxtaposition once common as domestic-scale buildings were progressively replaced by large Victorian warehouse buildings. The building's river elevation, with its oriel window of a type once common in Docklands, is rare and must be retained. The Town of Ramsgate once rejoiced in the name of The

Red Cow, and it was here that James II's notorious Lord Chancellor Jeffreys, whose trials and executions had shocked the country, was caught in 1688 when he tried to flee the country on the downfall of his royal master. The judge was recognised by a man he had bullied in court. Jeffreys begged to go to prison to save himself from the multitude after his blood. He was taken to the Tower where he later died.

The Gun at Blackwall, Isle of Dogs, is of some antiquity, being shown on pre-1800 maps of the area. This appears to be a timber-framed building of which the structure could date back to the 17th Century, although the present cladding is of the 19th Century. A less well known pub is The Ferry House, also on the Isle of Dogs, an intriguing building with a tower from which it is said a watch was kept for the ferry from Greenwich. The present building probably dates from 1822 but there appears to have been a tavern on the site from a much earlier period. This is a building with great potential which must be retained.

In the Royal Docks are three splendid old English type hotel/pubs, all formerly built by the dock company and leased to breweries. They are The Connaught Tavern, The Central Buffet and The Galleons Hotel. The Connaught's claim to fame is twofold. Just outside is a urinal, now listed: called by generations of 'Royal' dockers the 'Iron Lung', it is one of the few cast-iron Victorian urinals left in London. In front of The Connaught's balcony, on the right-hand side of the entrance to the Royal Victoria Dock, was 'The Stump'. Here, on the remains of a large tree, dockers' leaders and the unofficial shop stewards' committees addressed mass meetings. The stump was removed a couple of years ago.

All three of these buildings were designed by Vigers and Wagstaffe in the 1880s and all are now owned by the Corporation. It is hoped that new uses will be found for them.

The Central Buffet

The Gun

The Connaught Tavern

The Galleons Hotel

The Prospect of Whitby

The Town of Ramsgate

Wapping Pierhead

Interior, Wapping Pierhead

Newell Street

Isle House

Houses

Many years of indiscriminate clearance have unfortunately reduced Docklands' stock of early houses to a very low level. All surviving houses of the 18th and 19th Centuries which have been identified have now been listed, and because of their rarity will be given careful attention when applications for listed building consents for alterations are received.

Apart from Nelson House (the 18th Century shipbuilder's house at Nelson Dockyard described earlier), the finest houses in Docklands are probably the two terraces at either side of the former entrance to the London Dock at Wapping Pierhead. These were designed by Daniel Alexander in 1811 and combine the traditional Georgian domestic style with the austere detail of the warehouses.

Also of note are the two former dockmaster's houses at West India Docks – Bridge House and Isle House, the former by John Rennie and the latter by his son. These are both elegant detached houses with bowed frontages to the gardens, the former with an impressive Doric porch. Bridge House is to be converted into six flats. Adjacent to Isle House is Nelson House, Coldharbour, a distinguished late Georgian town house with a nice fanlighted front door, and next to this is a pair of lesser but pleasant Georgian houses, backing onto the river.

The best surviving terrace of riverside houses is that adjacent to The Grapes in Narrow Street. These are mostly mid-18th Century. Their street elevation is fairly original although the ground floors were once converted into shops. The riverside frontage has however been so severely altered that, with the exception of two houses, their historic character has been almost completely lost. Another good Georgian terrace survives in nearby Newell Street, Limehouse. The houses here are mostly original though many require attention. These houses still have good examples of Georgian door cases.

Many of the surviving houses in Docklands have suffered years of neglect, usually having been let to tenants on controlled rents. Gradually they are now coming into owner occupation and are being refurbished and restored.

Alterations and repairs or extensions, when permitted, must however be designed with special care and be of a quality of construction appropriate to a listed building. As most of these surviving houses are in prominent locations, the roof line is extremely important and roof extensions are unlikely to be permitted. Similarly, dormer windows invariably change the architectural character of the roofs and, if permitted at all, will be required to be of a design appropriate to the design of the building. Internally, it is accepted that a degree of re-

ordering will usually be necessary particularly to accommodate the domestic services required today. Again, however, it will be expected that the essential plan form will be retained, together with surviving historic features such as doors, panelling, fireplaces and cornices.

Owners will be encouraged to carry out suitable restorations using appropriate materials and to put back missing features such as panelled doors, sash windows, stone parapets, railings etc. The historic building grants which may be available to assist restoration work are described at Appendix 1.

Nelson House, Coldharbour

Narrow Street

Bridge House

Architectural Neighbours

Development work is also being carried out in and around a number of important historic buildings on the fringes of Docklands, many of which form part of conservation areas adjoining London Docklands' boundaries. The history of sites such as Greenwich, Woolwich and the Royal Arsenal has been closely bound up with the development of the Port of London and Docklands, and they still have an important impact on the area's environment.

Close by the Tower of London, the site of the Royal Mint (which in the 16th Century served as a naval victualling yard) is now to be redeveloped but its dignified buildings by James Johnson and Sir Robert Smirke dating from 1810 are to be restored. Some 500 years earlier, the Cistercians had built the abbey of St. Mary Graces there and significant parts of its structure have been excavated. These will be incorporated and displayed in the new development by the Crown Estate Commissioners. On the south side of the river at Deptford's naval victualling yard is a group of fine rum warehouses fronting onto the river. The refurbishment of these warehouses, carried out by the London County Council in the early 1960s, was one of the first imaginative restorations of such structures to have been undertaken.

Mention has already been made of the Royal Foundation of St. Katharine and the importance for environmental, social and historic reasons that the LDDC attaches to it. The Foundation stands on the northern side of the Thames at St. James' Ratcliffe, in the area between Butcher Row (which connects The Highway with Commercial Road, the northern approach road of the Rotherhithe Tunnel) and the viaduct of the old London and Blackwall Railway (now the new Docklands Railway).

Although it did not come to the site till 1948 (when it moved from the bomb blasted Bromley Hall in Poplar) its history has been closely bound to that of Docklands, which its fortunes and misfortunes have echoed.

Founded by Queen Matilda in 1147 as a medieval hospital next to the Tower of London, the Foundation stood at the east end of the creek which became known as 'Katharine's Dock.' Here for over six hundred years it quietly carried out its work as a chapter of an ecclesiastical college, becoming increasingly concerned with the care of the infirm and sick. But in June of 1825 the St. Katharine Dock Act was passed, the medieval church was destroyed and the Foundation removed to Regent's Park, until it returned to the East End at Bromley Hall in 1914. In June 1944 the chapter proposed that its future work in the East End should be *given to a scheme of social work and training operating from a community centre on a religious basis with a residential settlement,* and in 1948 it returned to its present site close to the Thames at St. James' Ratcliffe.

The Victorian church of St. James' had been destroyed by bombing, but the handsome Georgian vicarage was restored as the House of the Warden or Master – Father St. John Groser. This was to be the centre of a community of priests and women workers dedicated to religious and social service and to the care of the elderly. The original Master's House was built in 1796 by Matthew Whiting, a wealthy sugar importer, on the site of an earlier house which was burnt when fire consumed the adjacent Shipwrights Hall in 1794. Matthew Whiting's house is a well proportioned yet unpretentious brick Georgian house, given in its interior a surprising though pleasing quality by the large mural paintings covering whole walls in the principal rooms on the garden front.

The wall paintings are of landscapes which might be described as in the manner of Claude by way of Richard Wilson. It is not known who the painter was – perhaps an amateur friend of Whiting or an ambitious young apprentice? The enigma of authorship is there for future young art historians to unravel. Suffice it to say here that in their scope and scale they are unique wall paintings to have survived intact in a merchant's house of the 18th Century.

A new chapel was designed for the Foundation by R E Enthoven in 1950 together with community buildings,

Rum Warehouses, Deptford

Artist's Impression of Abbey of St. Mary Graces Excavation Works

a refectory, conference hall and rooms for visitors. With its pergolas and brick paved walks, the whole forms a cloistral enclosure of charming and peaceful gardens. Memorial tablets from the ancient church and others from Regent's Park line the outer wall of the south cloister, and outside the chapel is a sculptured stone panel of the nativity, salvaged from the bombed ruins of the Master's House of Regent's Park. Statues of Edward III and Queen Philippa stand at the entrance to the chapel, which contains the splendid 14th Century choir stalls from the medieval church and the magnificently carved 17th Century hexagonal pulpit bearing four views of the ancient hospital, with the outer and inner gate. These finely crafted works are blended with modern work by Keith Murray and a Christ in Majesty of Burma teak by Michael Groser.

The area around the Royal Foundation today is one of decay and dereliction, but also of resurgence. The new railway to the north is nearing completion. Demolished and obsolete tenaments to the east could provide land for development, perhaps in a form that could enable an extension of the social caring work of the Foundation. Sheltered housing for the elderly and the handicapped could also extend in a physical form this 'urban oasis' which has so uniquely survived the changing fortunes of Docklands.

Royal Foundation of St. Katharine – Matthew Whiting's House

Royal Foundation of St. Katharine – Wall Paintings

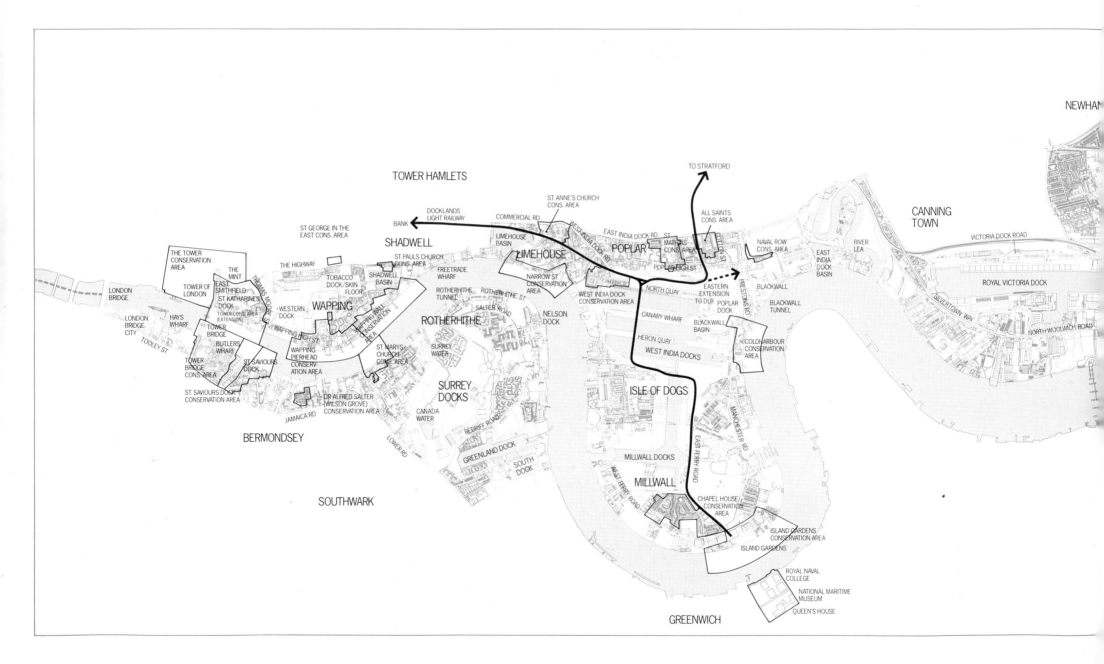

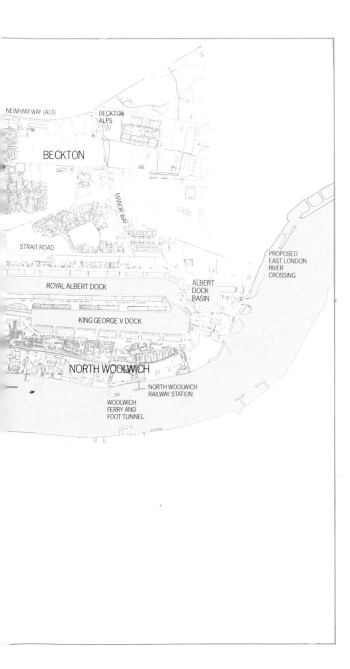

Conservation Areas

The LDDC inherited ten conservation areas from the Borough Councils of Tower Hamlets and Southwark in 1981 (two of which it has since extended) and has itself designated a further seven since. It has also identified an additional six areas (some of them extensions of existing conservation areas) which it regards as being of architectural and historical interest meriting further study.

Designated Conservation Areas

The seventeen designated conservation areas in Docklands are:

Conservation Areas Inherited from Borough Councils
Tower Hamlets
>**The Tower Conservation Area** designated outstanding January 1980
>**Wapping Pierhead Conservation Area** designated outstanding January 1979
>**St. Anne's Church Conservation Area, Limehouse** designated outstanding December 1979
>**Narrow Street Conservation Area, Limehouse**
>**Coldharbour Conservation Area, Isle of Dogs**
>**Island Gardens Conservation Area, Isle of Dogs**

Southwark
>**Tower Bridge Conservation Area** designated outstanding October 1978 (extended December 1985)
>**St. Saviour's Dock Conservation Area** designated outstanding October 1978 (extended December 1985)

Dr. Alfred Salter (Wilson Grove) Conservation Area
St. Mary's Conservation Area, Rotherhithe
designated outstanding November 1975

Conservation Areas Designated by the LDDC
Tower Hamlets
>**Wapping Wall Conservation Area**
>**St. Paul's Church Conservation Area, Shadwell**
>**West India Dock Conservation Area, Poplar**
>**Chapel House Conservation Area, Isle of Dogs**
>**St. Matthias Conservation Area, Poplar**
>**All Saints Conservation Area, Poplar**
>**Naval Row Conservation Area, East India Dock**

The size and character of these conservation areas, described in geographical sequence in the following pages, is enormously varied, illustrating Docklands' rich architectural and environmental inheritance.

The maps on the following pages are colour-coded to show:

☐ Conservation areas

▨ Grade I listed buildings

▨ Grade II listed buildings

▨ Locally listed buildings

☐ Ecclesiastical buildings

All maps are 1:1250.

The Tower
of
London

Royal
Mint

CARTWRIGHT ST

CROFTS ST

JOHN FISHER ST

EAST   SMITHFIELD

TOWER BRIDGE APPROACH

ST. KATHARINE'S WAY

St. Katharine Docks

Ivory House

THOMAS MORE STREET

MEWS STREET

ST. ANTHONY'S CLOSE

BURR CLOSE

ST. KATHARINE'S WAY

Tower Bridge

River Thames

REDMEAD LANE

HERMITAGE WALL

ORION ST

HIGH ST

WAPPING HIGH ST

The Tower Conservation Area

The Tower of London itself lies outside the LDDC's boundaries. The part of the Tower Conservation Area which lies within Docklands takes in the land between Tower Bridge and Thomas More Street and includes the whole of the St. Katharine Docks. Many of the very fine old dock buildings have regrettably been demolished, but the Ivory House and the Dockmaster's House remain, and are listed Grade II.

The docks are currently being redeveloped by St. Katharine-by-the-Tower Limited. With their water areas now protected and used for moorings for different types of craft (cabin cruisers, yachts and Thames barges as well as historic ships) an extremely attractive and popular environment has been created, providing wide access for the public.

The St. Katharine Docks

Aerial View of the Tower Conservation Area

47

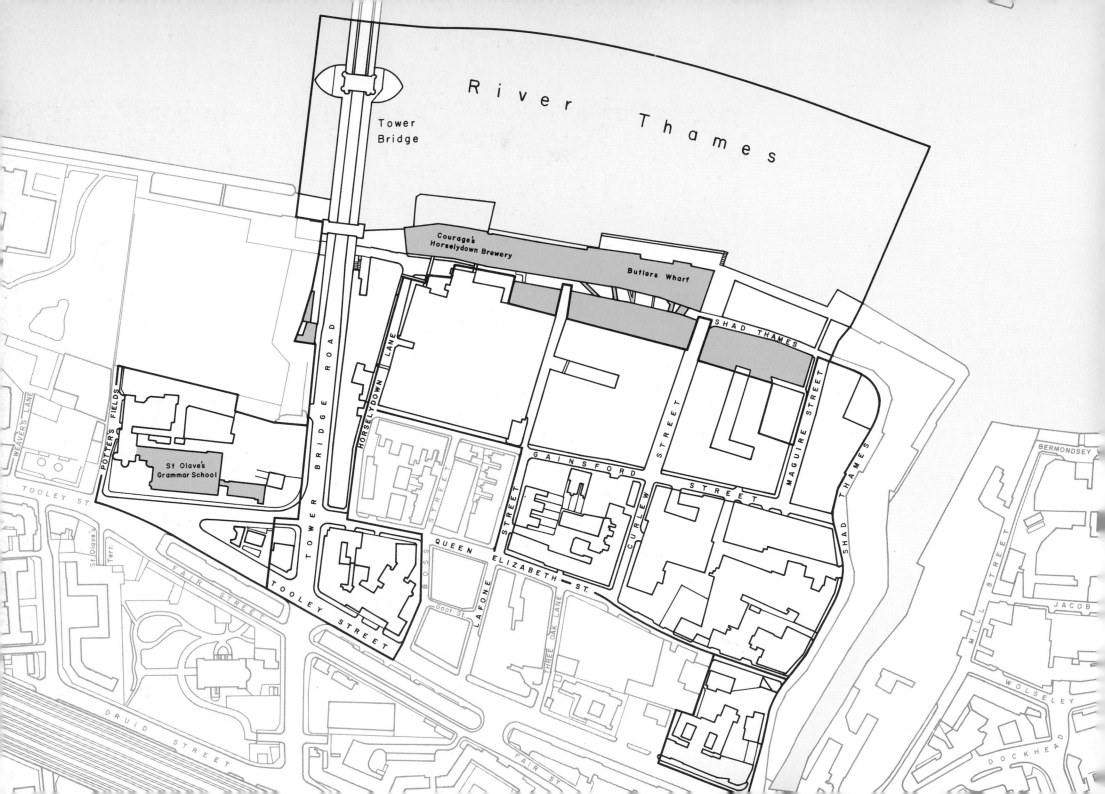

River Thames

Tower Bridge

Courage's Horselydown Brewery

Butlers Wharf

SHAD THAMES

POTTER'S FIELDS

St Olave's Grammar School

TOWER BRIDGE ROAD

HORSELYDOWN LANE

BOSS STREET

GAINSFORD STREET

CURLEW STREET

MAGUIRE STREET

SHAD THAMES

WEAVER'S LANE

TOOLEY ST.

St. Olave's Terr.

FAIR STREET

TOOLEY STREET

QUEEN ELIZABETH ST.

LAFONE STREET

Goat St.

THREE OAK LANE

FAIR ST.

DRUID STREET

BERMONDSEY STREET

MILL STREET

JACOB

WOLSELEY

DOCKHEAD

Tower Bridge Conservation Area

The Tower Bridge Conservation Area, the neighbouring St. Saviour's Dock Conservation Area and the area from Tooley Street to London Bridge, have been described as the only part of London (with the possible exception of Wapping) in which the Victorian character survives as a significant entity.

Designated 'outstanding' by the Department of the Environment in October 1978, the Tower Bridge Conservation Area takes in the approach to Tower Bridge on the south side, a row of small scale buildings which marks a strong contrast with the dramatic form of the bridge structure itself.

The area also includes the former main Courage's Brewery (once owned by the Theale family, friends of Dr Samuel Johnson) and the large warehouses of the Butler's Wharf Company. A great sense of drama is created by these large buildings which rise up on the bank of the Thames, enclosing and dwarfing narrow streets.

The Corporation has recently extended the conservation area to include the former St. Olave's school building, the remainder of the Butler's Wharf warehouses, a mid-19th Century spice mill, a Poor Law Guardians building and other buildings of character.

Butler's Wharf

St. Saviour's Dock Conservation Area

It is due to the very special character of St. Saviour's Dock and its buildings, most of which are now listed, that this conservation area was designated. Its one detracting feature is a lorry park, currently sited at the end of the eastern bank of the dock. It is hoped that, eventually, a new building will be erected here to complete the enclosure of the dock and enhance the entrance to Mill Street from the south.

The conservation area has recently been extended eastwards to include both sides of Mill Street, a number of interesting 19th Century buildings (some of which are listed) and the splendid Most Holy Trinity Church of 1960 by Goodhart-Rendel. Appropriate development will be encouraged to mould the area into a coherent whole.

The extension of the St. Saviour's Dock Conservation Area and that of the adjoining Tower Bridge Conservation Area will ensure that the atmosphere and character of Shad Thames and Mill Street are protected. The newly designated whole (i.e. the original St. Saviour's Dock and Tower Bridge Conservation Areas and their extensions) contains the best surviving groups of 19th Century warehouses in a street setting in Docklands and their conservation is of the greatest importance.

Aerial View of St. Saviour's Dock

St. Saviour's Dock

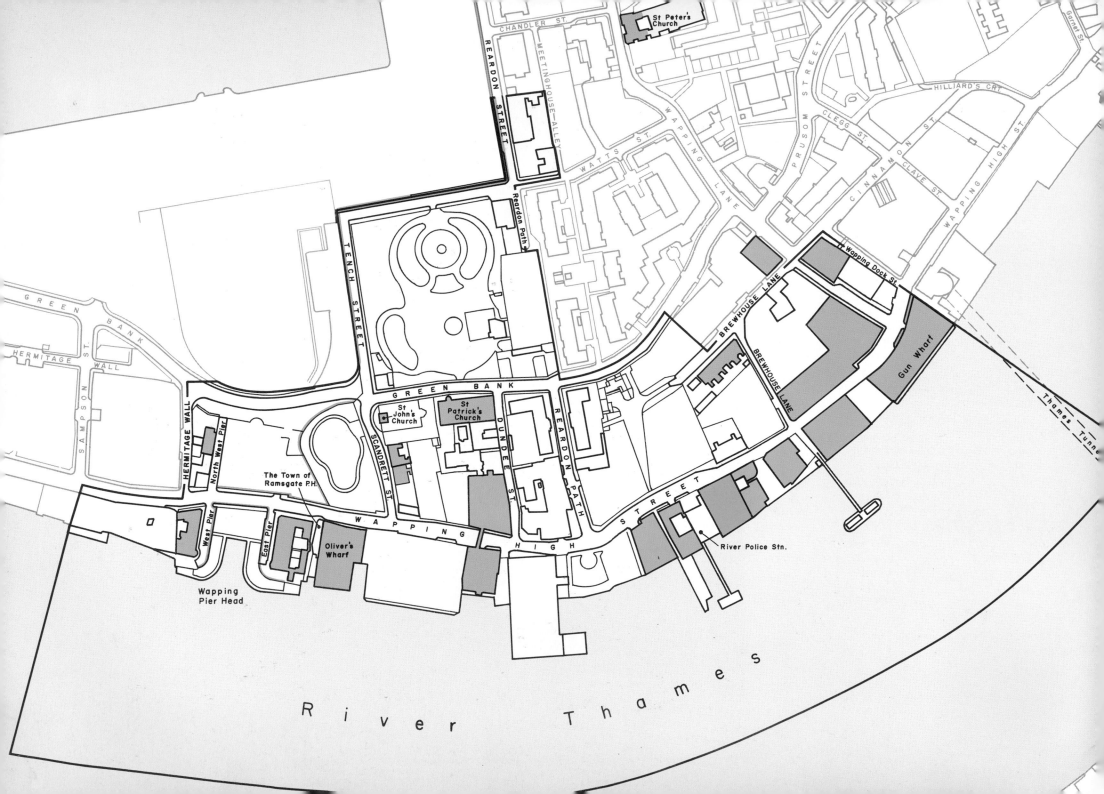

Wapping Pierhead Conservation Area

The name of this conservation area is derived from the former entrance to the London Dock. The original lock was filled in many years ago, but the LDDC is funding a paved landscaping scheme which follows its form. The superb terraces of houses on either side of the lock, built in 1811 for dock officials, are still there, and are one of the finest windows onto the river in Docklands. The London Borough of Tower Hamlets is rehabilitating the houses, and building new flats in the style of the original buildings on either side of the new open space. The area also includes four public open spaces in which it is intended that landscaping improvements be carried out.

The most important landmark in the area – the tower of the 18th Century church of St. John's, is in Scandrett Street. The nave of the church was mostly destroyed in the war: now derelict, it could provide a delightful garden within the ruined walls.

Alongside and opposite the old churchyard is the former schoolhouse (based on an earlier schoolhouse) with two entrances, above which small statues of a boy and girl still exist behind a corrugated iron protective hoarding. The later school building of 1797 has lost its roof and is in much worse condition than the original schoolhouse. The Corporation has tried unsuccessfully to arrange a restoration scheme with the owner and will now have to consider using its powers to ensure that these important historic buildings are restored and brought into active use.

The other buildings within this conservation area are mostly warehouses, some of which have already been converted into flats. There are proposals for the redevelopment of other warehouses and of most of the vacant sites in the area which, when carried out, will bring about a dramatic improvement in the environment.

Aerial View of Wapping Pierhead Conservation Area

Shadwell Basin

Brussels Wharf

GLAMIS RD.

Shadwell Pierhead

MILK YARD

WINE CLO.

GARNET STREET

WINE CLO.

MONZA ST.

Wapping Hydraulic Pumping Stn.

AGATHA CLO.

PEARL ST.

PENANG ST.

PRUSOM STREET

WAPPING WALL

Prospect of Whitby P.H.

Metropolitan Wharf

River Thames

New Crane Wharf

HILLIARD'S CRT.

CLEGG ST.

CINNAMON ST.

CLAVE ST.

WAPPING HIGH STREET

WAPPING LANE

Wapping Dock St.

Thames T

ROTHERHITHE

Wapping Wall Conservation Area

Immediately downstream from Wapping Pierhead, the Wapping Wall Conservation Area takes in the remainder of Wapping High Street and Wapping Wall, and the former entrance lock to the London Dock.

The major group of buildings within it are the large late 19th Century warehouses at New Crane Wharf and Metropolitan Wharf. Metropolitan Wharf was damaged by fire and is being sensitively repaired: it will continue in use as studio/workshops. New uses are being sought for the remaining warehouses in the group. Two of the smaller ones have already been granted planning permission for conversion into housing. A major refurbishment is planned for New Crane Wharf. New infill buildings are to be constructed on the small vacant sites facing onto Wapping High Street, with a linear courtyard – probably the original route of Wapping Wall – providing a new pedestrian route and access to the river.

Also within the Wapping Wall Conservation Area is the listed hydraulic pumping station which the LDDC and the Academy of St. Martin-in-the-Fields are planning to convert into recording and rehearsal studios, a restaurant and a small museum of pumping machinery.

Within the conservation area as a whole a great deal of redevelopment is taking place which, together with the refurbishment of existing buildings, will result in a complete upgrading of the environment. The Corporation is anxious to ensure that new buildings relate closely to the urban qualities of existing development and are built of materials traditional to the area.

Aerial View of Wapping Wall Conservation Area

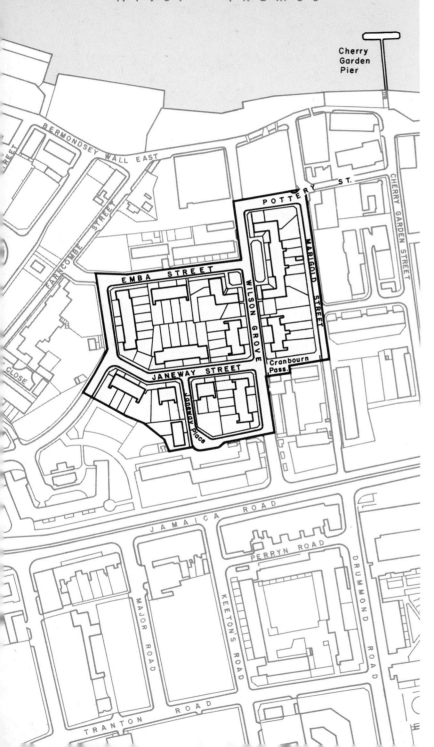

Dr. Alfred Salter (Wilson Grove) Conservation Area

This is a small estate of attractive cottage-style Council dwellings forming pleasant groupings. Now that Council tenants have the right to buy their homes, it can be expected that a number of these pleasant homes will become privately owned. It would greatly assist new owner-occupiers, many of whom are likely to want to improve and individualise their homes, if some form of design guide were available to help them do so, and the Corporation is giving consideration to a possible publication of this kind. Otherwise, it is feared that 'improvements' could destroy the harmony of the area, especially if high pressure salesmen of home improvement companies – many of whom have little understanding of traditional forms – are successful in their attempts to persuade new owners to carry out what may well be inappropriate modifications. Should this begin to happen, the LDDC may need to make an Article 4 direction and require owners to apply for planning permissions for alterations out of character with the conservation area. (See Appendix 2.)

St. Paul's Church Conservation Area, Shadwell

Centred around the 1820s church of St. Paul's, this small conservation area provides a dramatic backdrop to Shadwell Basin. The Corporation has recently funded the cleaning of the church and the former Church Institute, together with the improvement of the churchyard and the restoration of its railings. A row of attractive early 19th Century cottages facing the churchyard has been restored by a private owner and a grant from the LDDC has enabled its important front elevation, partially demolished by fire, to be restored to its original appearance.

Waterside housing is being developed around Shadwell Basin, which is used as a water sports training centre for young people under the direction of the East London Marine Venture. The churchyard is likely to become important as a through route when a flight of steps – which forms part of the Corporation's environmental improvement to the Basin and the churchyard, is constructed to the quayside. Full public access to the quayside and the harbour-like landscaping of Brussels Wharf will be an important element in the redevelopment scheme.

View of St. Paul's Church and Shadwell Basin

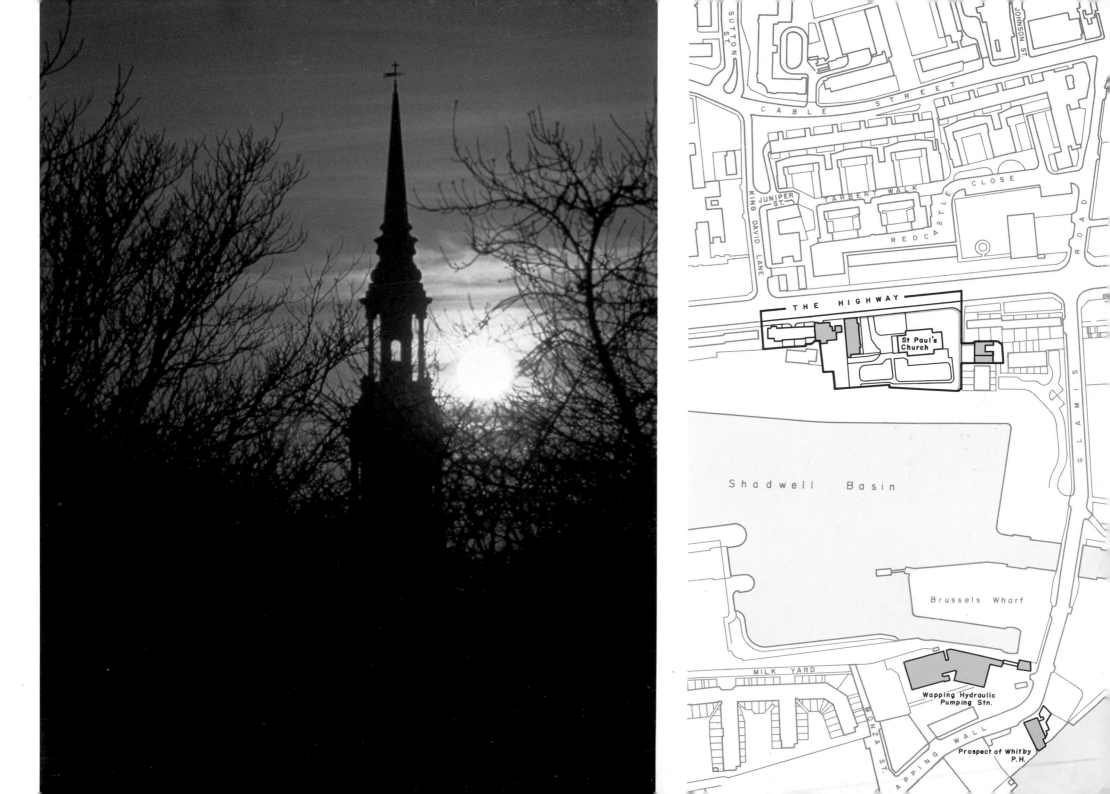

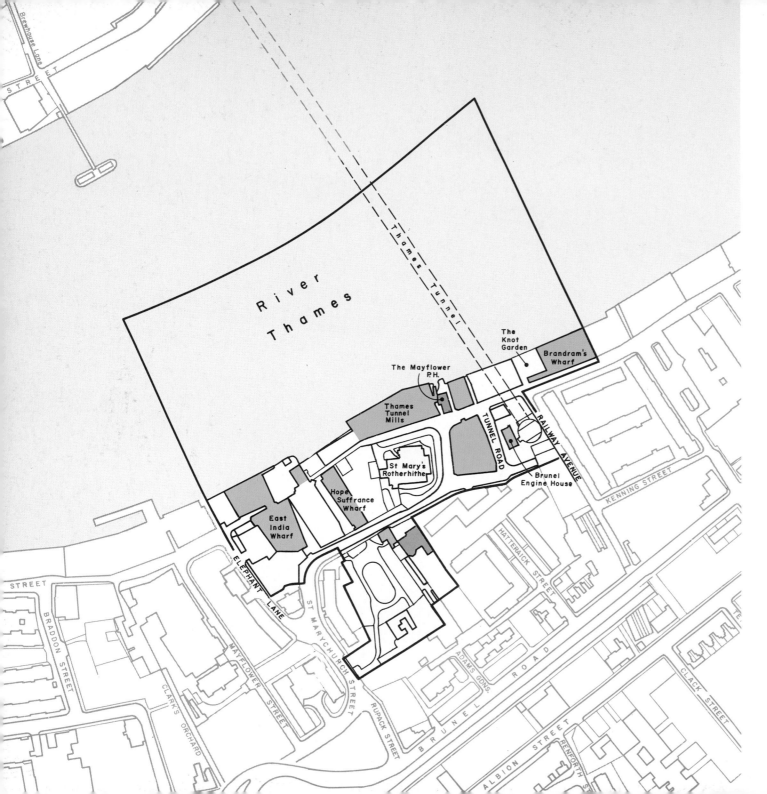

St. Mary's Conservation Area, Rotherhithe

The early 18th Century church of St. Mary's is the centrepiece of this particularly attractive conservation area. Opposite is the rectory, adjacent to which is the delightful little 18th Century schoolhouse. This was formerly a house and it still has its original timber panelling throughout. The front elevation is a lovely composition of panelled brickwork and has the traditional statues of a boy and girl set on brackets at first floor level. A key building in the conservation area, its survival has been assured by a generous grant for its repair by the Amicable Society. Next to this is a small park which has on the street frontage a former fire engine house and watch-house.

Along the river frontage are a number of large warehouse buildings, some of which have already been restored. One, Thames Tunnel Mills, has received a Civic Trust Award for its imaginative conversion by the London & Quadrant Housing Association, assisted by a grant from the Historic Buildings Council. The same housing association is also currently restoring Brandram's Wharf, a derelict warehouse at the eastern end of the conservation area. At the western end is a large complex of warehouses called East India Wharf, currently empty and derelict. Formerly owned by the GLC, it is hoped it will be sold to a sympathetic developer who will bring it back into use, and upgrade the environment.

Another historically important building within the conservation area is the former boiler house for the pumps for the famous Thames Tunnel. Erroneously called the Brunel Engine House it was built by Marc Brunel, the father of Isambard Kingdom Brunel. Between and adjacent to this is the shaft to the tunnel which incorporated the base of the former entrance building. This has been capped off and is now extremely ugly. It has been suggested that an improvement scheme involving the re-creation of the former tunnel entrance building could be carried out.

In front of these buildings is a paved open space. On the riverside is the Knot Garden (currently in need of repair), which has large rope sculptures set in cobblestones, and at Hope Sufferance Wharf is another small space. These spaces, which are important 'windows on the river', might benefit from an improvement scheme: a few trees might provide a welcome contrast of texture.

St. Anne's Church Conservation Area, Limehouse

The historic St. Anne's Church with its lovely churchyard of mature trees, lies at the centre of this conservation area. The western approach to the church is along a narrow cobbled lane leading straight to the main entrance stairs. This is most spectacular, the huge scale of the church standing in sharp contrast to the modestness of the approach lane. At its other end, the lane leads into Newell Street which has a terrace of listed 18th Century houses, many of which need external improvements and repairs.

Environmental improvements are being carried out in the area alongside the church and the nearby Regent's Canal. A derelict open space called King's Wharf between Newell Street and the Cut has recently been landscaped by the LDDC to provide an attractive route to the canal, as has the former rectory garden on the opposite side of the canal. The old London and Blackwall Railway viaduct, which lies at the southern boundary of the conservation area, is being refurbished to carry the Docklands Light Railway. It is hoped that external improvements to the Newell Street houses will also be undertaken, once environmental work, the refurbishment of the railway viaduct, and the development of Limehouse Basin beside which it runs, have taken more positive shape.

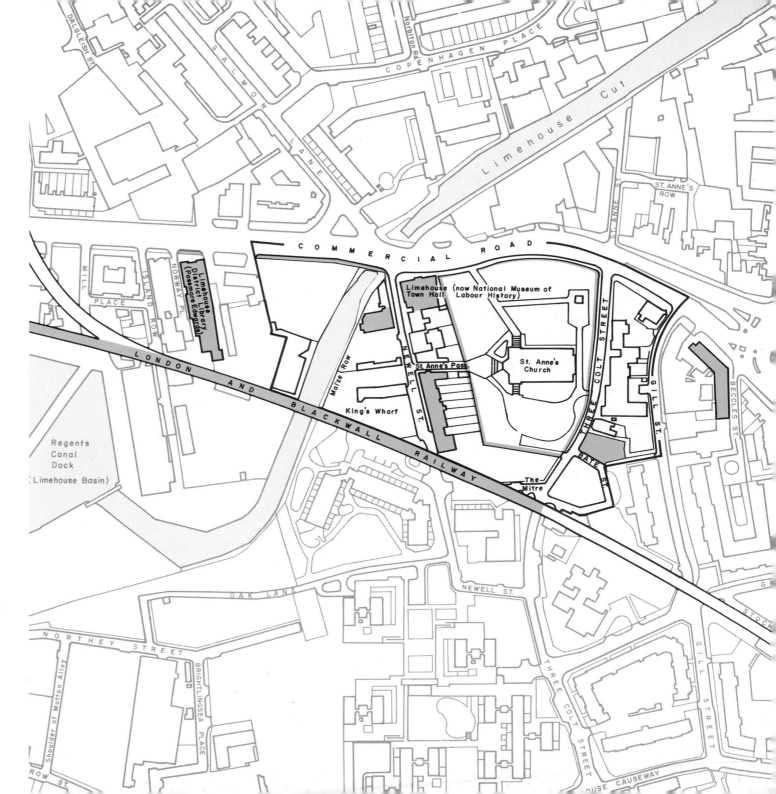

Narrow Street Conservation Area, Limehouse

The historic river front of Limehouse has attracted the attention of painters, engravers and photographers for over a hundred years. At its centre is an historic terrace of 18th Century houses, at one end of which is The Grapes public house, and at the other a former barge yard. The terrace is now an almost unique survivor of 18th Century riverside development, though many of the houses on the riverside have unfortunately had their character destroyed by the insertion of ill-designed large new windows; a few, however, remain unaltered, and particular attention will be paid to ensuring their preservation. The street elevation of the terrace generally remains unaltered. Narrow Street still retains much of its 19th Century atmosphere and one of its major disfiguring gaps – the vacant riverside site adjoining The Grapes – has recently been developed with houses which respect the scale and line of the old street frontage.

To the east of this, separated by two buildings, is the site of a former refuse depot which has been the subject of an architectural competition. The proposed redevelopment will continue the present street frontage and will include the reconstruction of a derelict Georgian house on the corner of the site. Further east lies Limekiln Dock, itself listed, along the north side of which is a group of listed warehouses which form part of Dunbar Wharf, named after the famous 19th Century shipowner, Duncan Dunbar. East of this again are three wharves with modern buildings. One of these has now been cleared and is being developed: the scheme will incorporate the restoration of the listed front doorway of the former Limehouse Kiln, erected in 1705.

The western boundary of the conservation area is formed by the entrance lock to the Regent's Canal Dock. Nearby is Hough's Paper and Board Mill, part of which falls outside the present conservation area boundary. This large, impressive Victorian industrial building should be retained and refurbished. Narrow Street Conservation Area is to be extended westwards to include the group of warehouses and to the north to take in other buildings and spaces of interest. The old dock entry and cottages have already been protected from demolition by Corporation action.

Limehouse was threatened some years ago by a proposal of the former GLC to drive a 'Northern Relief Road' through its heart. The LDDC prevented that environmental catastrophe and proposed an alternative route involving West India Dock Road and Commercial Road. The very success of the LDDC's plans to regenerate Docklands has once again created the need for a new east-west road not just to replace, but to augment, the existing A13 route into central London. Now the LDDC is considering how a road in tunnel and cut and cover construction through Limehouse could avoid destruction of the urban fabric and minimise its environmental impact.

Narrow Street

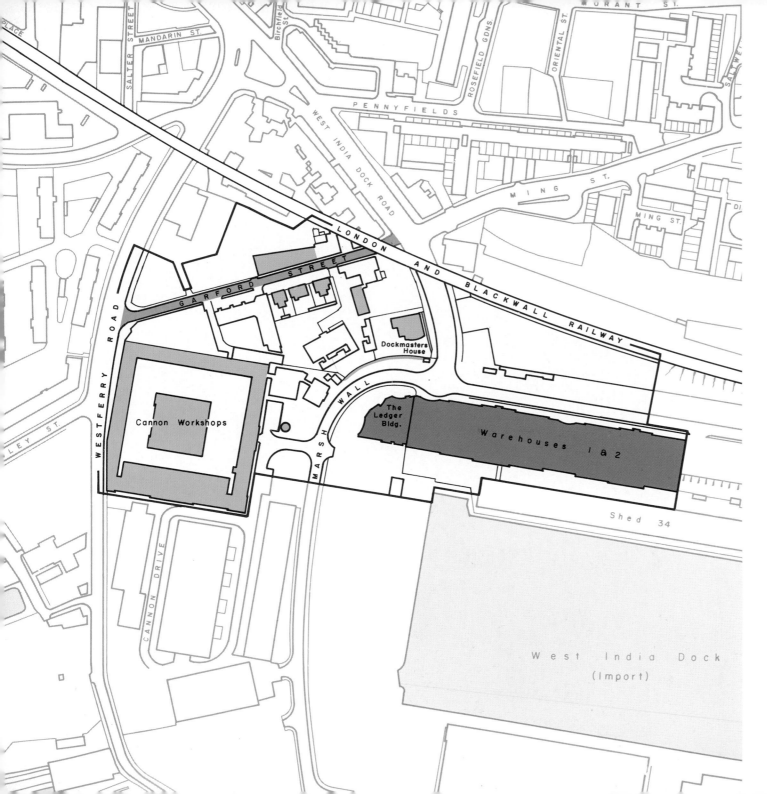

West India Dock Conservation Area, Isle of Dogs

This conservation area contains the last major group of buildings built by the West India Dock Company: they form the main entrance to the Isle of Dogs Enterprise Zone from the north. These Grade I listed buildings are of outstanding importance, and some first aid – including major repairs to the former dock offices or Ledger Building – has been carried out. The nearby Cannon Workshops, a group of former storehouses and workshops of 1824-25, have recently been cleaned and repaired, and the former Dockmaster's House (which enjoyed a period as a tavern) has been refurbished by the Corporation, as have the railings to its boundary. An even more interesting scheme to adapt the building for a quality restaurant which

Statue of Robert Milligan

involves the restoration of the original colonnaded porch is now being considered.

When the new road access to the Enterprise Zone has been provided, the length of West India Dock Road between the railway bridge and the entrance to the Enterprise Zone will be pedestrianised. The LDDC has already restored the gate piers on either side of the entrance. It proposes in due course to rebuild the middle gate pier and to provide new gates to match those taken away not much more than ten years ago. The ground in front of the warehouses is to be paved (as has been done at

the west end of the Ledger Building) and the statue of Robert Milligan – presently held in safe-keeping by the Museum of London – is to be set up in front of the Ledger Building where it was first erected in 1810.

The conservation area extends northwards to the railway viaduct, and takes in Garford Street. This street has the last remaining row of dock constables' cottages, fortunately in a good state of repair. On the opposite side of the street lies a derelict Victorian warehouse which is now listed, the restoration of which the Corporation will seek to secure, having succeeded in preventing demolition in 1983.

It is the Corporation's intention to use the listed warehouses and the adjacent Ledger Building, together with part of Shed 34 – a robust dockside warehouse of the 1930s, as the core of a major tourist development, Port East. To mark the western gateway of Port East, it is proposed to reconstruct the entrance arch, surmounted by a model of a West Indiaman merchant ship. The arch will lead on to the North Quay of the West India Import Dock.

Original entrance arch to the West India Docks – the 'Hibbert Gate'

Artist's Impression of Port East – showing proposed reconstruction of the 'Hibbert Gate'

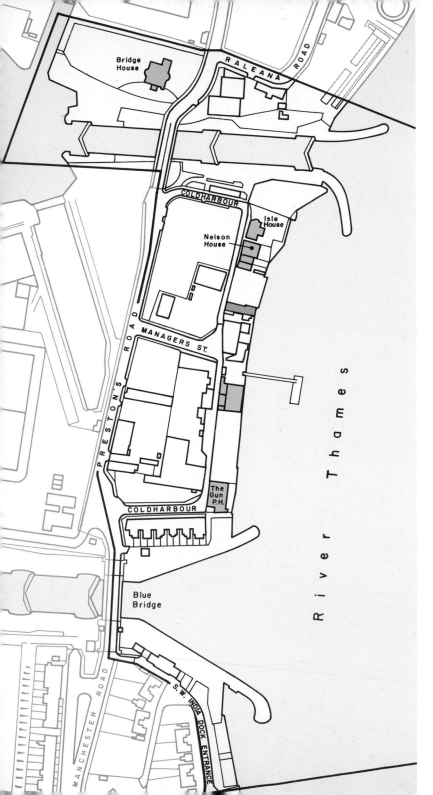

Coldharbour Conservation Area, Isle of Dogs

The major elements in the Coldharbour Conservation Area are the former Blackwall Entrance Lock to the West India Docks (which was reconstructed in its present form in 1895) and the handsome Bridge House built for the dock superintendant in 1819 by John Rennie. The area is currently being redeveloped with waterside housing around Blackwall Basin: more new housing is to be built to the east of the existing road bridge over the lock. The bridge itself is being replaced by a causeway to relieve chronic traffic congestion, and to allow views into the lock and basins.

To the south of the lock lies Coldharbour, almost the last surviving example of the very narrow streets which once ran parallel to the river. Unfortunately, Coldharbour is subject to a road widening line and it is likely that its historic character will be eroded, unless the LDDC and the Borough Council are able to agree that the area merits special consideration and that a more appropriate solution should be sought.

At the north end of Coldharbour is the Isle House of 1825, also designed by Sir John Rennie. To the south of this are Nelson House and a pair of early 19th Century terraced houses, all of which are listed. Also in Coldharbour is the old police station and the historic Gun public house and a row of 19th Century cottages which run parallel to the west entrance lock. The modern yet striking Dutch-style Blue Bridge is only partly within the conservation area, but the historic river entrances to a pair of ancient drydocks (now filled in) are included.

The Coldharbour Conservation Area is about to undergo great changes, with the planned redevelopment of derelict land within and close to it. The Corporation will insist on a high standard of design for the new developments to ensure that they will enhance, and not detract from, the area.

Island Gardens Conservation Area, Isle of Dogs

This conservation area is centred around the historic Island Gardens which were formed out of a reed ground at the end of the 19th Century. This is a most cherished piece of open space, taking in as it does the famous view of the Royal Naval College and the Queen's House at Greenwich. The gardens are also an important space in their own right, having a large number of well developed trees.

To the east of the gardens is a new housing development, and to the east of this is Newcastle Draw Dock, a listed structure, where barges would formerly have been unloaded at low tide. Next to this is Cumberland Mills (a former oilseed mill), most of which has been demolished. In Glenafric Avenue lies the listed Waterman's Arms and the impressive silhouette of Christ Church, whose spire is a major local landmark.

The conservation area extends northwards to Manchester Road and encompasses the George Green School. To the west of Island Gardens, it extends along the river bank as far as Ferry Street and The Ferry House public house. It also includes Johnson's Draw Dock which it is proposed will be re-opened as a public access to the river.

View of Greenwich Palace from Island Gardens

SPINDRIFT AVENUE

River Thames

Masthouse Terrace
(Napier Yard)

Burrell's Wharf

CAHIR STREET

MARSH ST.

HARBINGER ROAD

Harbinger Rd.
Primary
School

Millwall
Iron Works
(Part)

HESPERUS CRESCENT

THERMOPYLAE GATE

MACQUARIE WAY

Chapel
House
Estate

CHAPEL HOUSE STREET

JULIAN PL.

WEST FERRY ROAD

FERRY ROAD

EAST FERRY ROAD

Docklands
Settlement

Millwall Park

MANCHESTER GROVE

Millwall
Fire Stn.

MANCHESTER ROAD

The Lord Nelson P.H.

FERRY STREET

The
Ferry House
P.H.

Livingstone Pl.

Midland Pl.

Chapel House Conservation Area, Isle of Dogs

At the south end of the Isle of Dogs, the Chapel House Conservation Area includes three estates of cottages built by Poplar Borough Council in the 1920s and 1930s. These attractive cottage-style buildings are in pleasant surroundings; the Chapel House Estate itself lies in well-developed landscape. Also within the conservation area are three terraces of simple small scale houses of a type once common on the island.

As is the case with the Wilson Grove Conservation Area, Chapel House could benefit from design advice: there is some evidence that this would be appreciated by potential new homeowners in the area.

Cottage-style Housing in Chapel House Estate

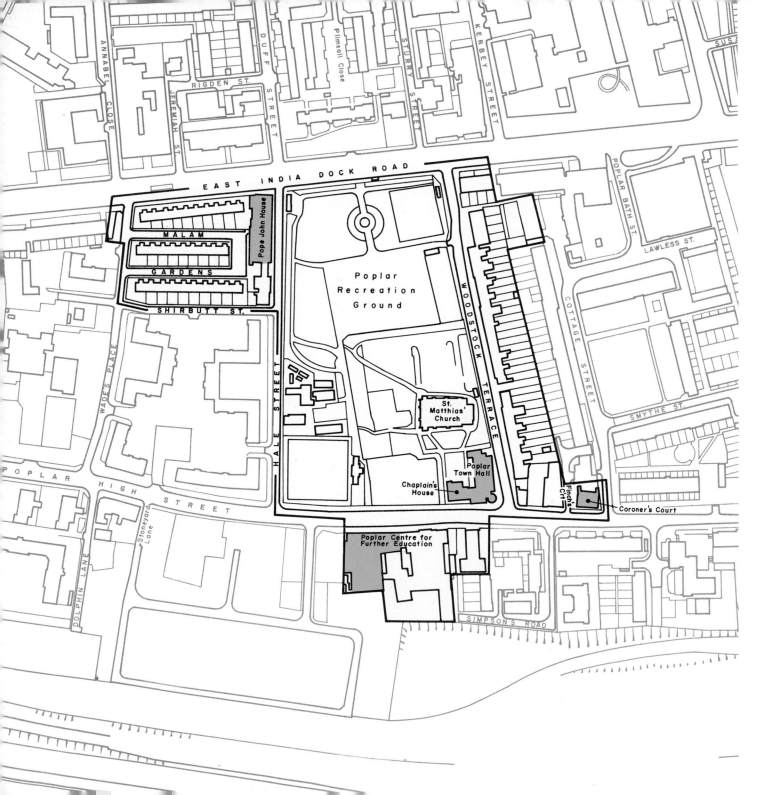

St. Matthias Conservation Area, Poplar

This conservation area has as its centrepiece the historic St. Matthias Church – the oldest building in Docklands, which the LDDC is acquiring to restore as a centre for the performing arts. Its churchyard still has much original charm. Around this is Poplar Recreation Ground. Both these landscapes have great potential for improvement. Proposals for this and for improved access to the church when restored will be implemented over the next few years.

Facing these open spaces are Woodstock Terrace (an attractive terrace of late 19th Century houses) and the Poplar Centre for Further Education (the former Poplar Technical College), a large listed educational building neatly faced in Portland stone, which is soon to be cleaned. At the junction of Woodstock Terrace and Poplar High Street is the charmingly picturesque Victorian former Poplar Town Hall, now refurbished as a local housing office. Next to this is the former East India Company's Chaplain's House.

The conservation area also includes the listed Coroner's Court, a free style Arts & Crafts building in the east, and Pope John House plus a small estate of former gas company cottages in the west.

The Former East India Company's Chaplain's House

All Saints Conservation Area, Poplar

All Saints Church was recently cleaned and repaired by the Corporation and forms a splendid focus for this conservation area. It is set in a large, generally well-maintained churchyard which has many mature trees. However, there is scope for landscaping improvement and the LDDC will be seeking to achieve this, together with the repair of the important table tombs. The rectory is a splendid large double fronted house of the same date as the church, set in a large garden. If the railings to the churchyard and rectory could be restored to their original pattern, of which a small portion still remains, it would be a great improvement to the character of the churchyard and a great enhancement of the area.

The conservation area also includes two good Georgian terraces, The Greenwich Pensioner public house and the Cotton Street open space, recently landscaped by the Corporation to provide an attractive setting for the church from the east.

All Saints Church, Rectory

Montague Place

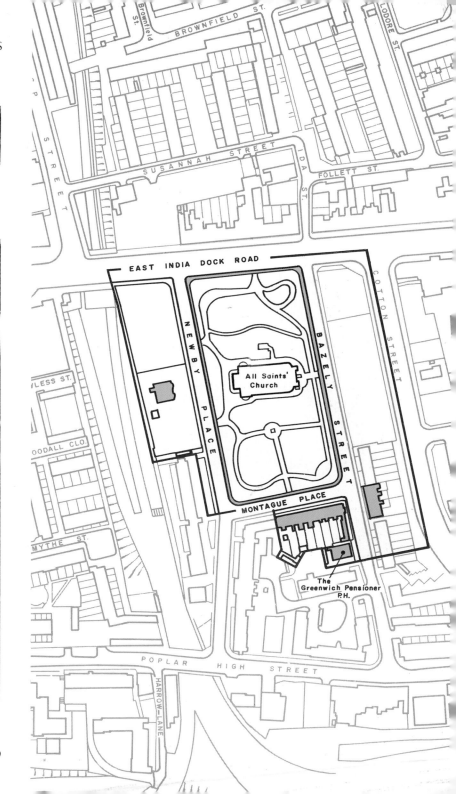

69

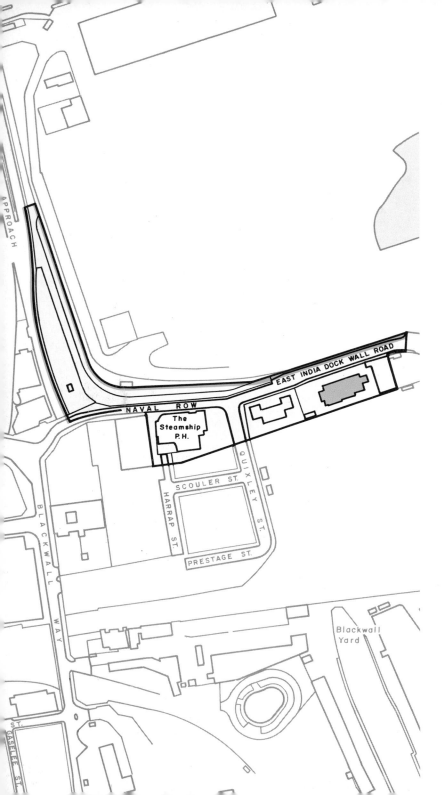

Naval Row Conservation Area, East India Docks

This conservation area lies in a partly forgotten area to the south of the East India Import Dock. The northern boundary is formed by the listed wall to the East India Docks, which is set in a narrow, well-wooded park for much of its length. Seen on a sunny day it is a delightful place, with the mature trees of the park providing an attractive foil to the wall, whose yellow and pink hues are enlivened by the moving shadows of the foliage. The road is set at a lower level than the park which is retained by another listed wall.

On the south side of the road opposite the park is The Steamship public house and a small, late-19th Century industrial building. To the east of this are the Naval Row flats which have recently been refurbished. They increase the sense of enclosure of the street and provide a visual link with the listed hydraulic pumping station, which is at the street's eastern end.

East India Import Dock Wall

Additional Areas of Architectural and Historic Interest

In addition to the officially designated conservation areas within Docklands there are six areas which the Corporation wishes to study further with a view to deciding whether designations as conservation areas are merited. These are:

Newham
  Royal Victoria Gardens, North Woolwich
  Royal Victoria Dock/Pontoon Dock, Silvertown –
  Silos and Warehouses.
Southwark
  Tooley Street, Bermondsey
  Nelson Dock/Rotherhithe Street/Acorn Estate,
  Southwark
  Church House, Downtown, Rotherhithe
  Lavender Lock, Southwark.

This list is not considered exhaustive: it is possible that other areas requiring conservation measures will be identified in future.

Tooley Street, Bermondsey

Tooley Street, extending from London Bridge to Tower Bridge and further east to St. Saviour's Dock, is the historic spine from which a number of narrow access roads served the wharves along the Bermondsey river front, and which provided an east/west connection to the two historic bridges. The coherence of the mostly Victorian buildings fronting onto the road provides a sense of historic continuity, and acts as a foil to the new buildings as has been well demonstrated in the London Bridge City development. It was this historic 'grain' in the pattern of development which the Inspector stressed in his report on the Public Inquiry into the London Bridge City development in 1981.

At the west end of Tooley Street are a number of

large scale Victorian warehouses and the splendid Art Deco St. Olaf's House offices for Hays Wharf, designed by Goodhart-Rendel. Between this group and the now extended boundary of the Tower Bridge Conservation Area, the street provides a more or less continuous frontage of Victorian and Edwardian buildings, nearly all of which are of architectural quality and interest.

The southern end of Tooley Street also has buildings of interest, most of which would benefit from cleaning, as would the Tooley Street frontage of the railway viaduct. Mention should also be made of the railway bridges in the vicinity of London Bridge, whose recent repainting, following the cleaning of the St. Thomas Street façade of the viaduct, is a major environmental improvement.

The refurbishment of Hays Dock as a new 'Galleria,' of Emblem House and Chamberlains Wharf as a private hospital, and the restoration of St. Olaf's House, firmly anchor the area into that historic 'grain' referred to by the Secretary of State.

Royal Victoria Gardens, North Woolwich

The Royal Victoria Gardens, a pleasant park set by the riverside, were opened in May 1851 (the year of the Great Exhibition) as bait to tempt the Victorians to travel on the newly-built London and Blackwall railway line. Pleasure gardens in London had reached their peak in the 18th Century but were still a popular amusement for the Victorians. They had many, varied attractions – from baby shows to theatre, dancing, dining and of course balloon ascents. Indeed it is alleged that William Holland, one of the managers of the gardens, ran into financial trouble and escaped his creditors by taking flight in a balloon. (He later recouped his fortune by founding the Winter Gardens, Blackpool.) It is probable that George Parker Bidder, who built the railway line (and shortly afterwards the Royal Victoria Dock) was responsible for the Royal Victoria Gardens, designed as a rival to the famous Cremorne Gardens.

To the east of this seemingly tranquil local park lie two nice terraces of early 20th Century houses (in Bargehouse Road and Woolwich Manor Way), and the Victorian sewage pumping station. The river wall works at the end of these roads have destroyed links with the river but at the end of Bargehouse Road the old granite setted causeway remains on the foreshore.

To the west of the Royal Victoria Gardens is the police station, a well executed Edwardian design. Nearby is the North Woolwich Railway Station, recently restored by the Corporation, and the listed entrance to the Woolwich Foot Tunnel.

Royal Victoria Dock/Pontoon Dock, Silvertown – Silos and Warehouses

The area around the Pontoon Dock, which includes the surviving flour mills and silos, forms a distinct group of interesting industrial buildings. The Pontoon Dock itself was built in 1860 as a place where ships – lifted out of the water by the famous hydraulic ship lift and floated into the small finger docks – could be repaired on pontoons. Most of the docks have now been filled in but these could be re-excavated and would provide an attractive setting for new developments.

The flour mills and silos are an important landmark from many viewpoints and especially from over the dock. Examples of the later, more imperial, stage of Docklands history, they have an impressive sense of scale, greatly enhanced by their closeness to the water, and provide a very powerful architectural group. Perhaps the most interesting is the former CWS Mill, now owned by the LDDC. 'D' silo – with its octagonal cupola on top, is the most interesting architecturally, with an attractive profile and monumental form.

St. Olaf's House, Tooley Street

Canada Wharf

Columbia Wharf

Nelson Dock/Rotherhithe Street/Acorn Estate, Southwark

This historic area is composed of two elements, the oldest being the area of the historic Nelson Dock, the other the Acorn Estate.

In Nelson Dock is the handsome Nelson House, a Grade II listed building, an example of the more than modest comfort in which an 18th Century shipbuilder lived. Although now used as offices, it is kept in very good condition. The Dock also contains the dry dock slipway and 'patent slip' with its engine house. This is a most important survival of the industrial history of Docklands.

North of Nelson Dock are the late 19th Century Columbia Wharf, with Moorish style detailing in its brick arches, and Canada Wharf – bounded by Horn Stairs at Cuckolds Point. The frontage to Rotherhithe Street is varied and lively, comprising mostly 19th Century industrial brick buildings with simple detailing. The Blacksmith's Arms – a pub for shiprepair workers, is a jolly piece of 'Tudoresque' infill.

Across Rotherhithe Street the inland site consists of the Acorn Estate, one of the most interesting of the inter-war Downtown estates built by the old London County Council. A flat crescent of three four-storey blocks of brick and render and tile roof follows the line of Rotherhithe Street. Four short and a fifth double block enclose the large courtyard on the west side. This housing, until recently in poor condition, is now being refurbished for a mixture of rental and owner occupation by Barratt (East London) Limited.

Church House, Downtown, Rotherhithe

This small area is characterised by the Holy Trinity Church and its vicarage with spacious walled garden, the church hall, and the blocks of flats known as Church House and Bryan House. These buildings are in the characteristic striped Bermondsey housing style. The recent refurbishment of Church House by Barratts (East London) Limited shows how attractive they can be with their strong bands of red brick and red tile roofs.

The area is bounded to the west by the landscaped edge of the Salters Road highway (more tree planting along this boundary would make a significant improvement) and to the north by an attractive new housing scheme now under construction. The resurfacing of Bryan Road with paving blocks and additional tree planting would increase the attractiveness of this quiet corner of Downtown.

Lavender Lock, Southwark

Lavender Lock and its pumping station – a fine and dignified building of yellow stock bricks with gauged brick arches and slated roof – are set in a delightful landscape encompassing the old Lavender Pond. The lock itself was built in 1863 and provided access to Lavender Pond which was used for floating timber bulk storage. Rotherhithe Street now separates the lock from the pump house and the pond, but originally a small drawbridge spanned the lock.

Adjoining the site of the pump house is a pair of cottages in a simple modern vernacular style. Beyond them on the north side of Rotherhithe Street are three short terraces of Downtown cottages separated by two small blocks of Downtown style flats, desperately requiring refurbishment. The cottages, with their attractively planted front gardens, are delightful. Small treasures such as these are now being uncovered and restored throughout Docklands, as redevelopment work continues.

Enjoying the Docklands Heritage

The conservation of the Docklands heritage has to be seen as an essential part of its regeneration process, setting the scene for new developments as well as providing its own development opportunities. However there is also a great potential to encourage the exploration and enjoyment of the area by the local community, by visitors from London and further afield and by overseas tourists.

Access to London Docklands

Transport links between Docklands, central London and the rest of the country have already been greatly improved: facilities for road, rail, river and air services currently under construction or planning will complete the transport infrastructure of the area within the coming years. New roads and bus routes now lead into Docklands, particularly the Isle of Dogs and the Surrey Docks peninsula. Further roads are planned to provide links between the emerging developments in the Royal Docks and the Isle of Dogs, penetrating to the very heart of those docks to which public access has been denied for a century or more.

The new Docklands Light Railway – Britain's first – is due to open later in 1987, and will connect much of the area with London's underground railway system. Passing over, as well as through, a sequence of historic areas from the Tower of London to Island Gardens across the Thames from Greenwich, it will provide easy access as well as being an attraction in itself. From Island Gardens runs the foot tunnel to Greenwich – beloved of hooting children – with its Palace, Park and Observatory, the National Museum,

the 'Cutty Sark' and the Queen's House, Inigo Jones' bold architectural innovation that heralded a new style in English architecture. The new London City Airport in East Docklands, also due to open later in 1987, will provide air services to provincial cities in Britain and to European capitals and other continental cities. The Great East London River Crossing suspension bridge to be built at Galleons Reach – the eastern gateway to Docklands – will assuredly become as much a tourist attraction as that other great feat of 20th Century engineering, the Thames Barrier. On the river the construction of new piers and the renovation of old ones will provide access to a planned high speed river bus service from Tower Pier to Greenwich, whilst with the development of riverfront sites, new walks will be opened up along the riverside and docks.

Special Attractions

The St. Katharine Docks are already an established tourist attraction. It is expected that new developments will bring many more thousands of visitors to the area. The biggest of these is Port East, a proposed leisure and shopping complex centred on a number of listed warehouses in the West India Docks. Port East will contain shops, boutiques, craft workshops, a food hall, specialised restaurants and bars together with a Docklands museum gallery and exhibition space and an exhibition of historic ships. The converted warehouses, with glazed roof atria providing light in the very hearts of the buildings, will once again demonstrate the dignity and grandeur created by their

Limehouse Cut

The St. Katharine Docks

St. Matthias Church

Railway Viaduct over West India Dock

Tobacco Dock

original designers. A typical narrow Docklands street will link the quayside piazza outside the Ledger Building and Warehouse 1 with a new hotel complex. Dockside cranes and quayside spaces will bring the flavour of waterside history to the massive Canary Wharf financial development nearby and to the Chinese quarter with its planned China Trade Centre at Poplar Dock, east of the new Billingsgate Fish Market.

The shopping complex in the brick vaults and columned spaces of the Grade I listed Skin Floor, the proposed centre for the performing arts and music in the restored Baroque chapel of the East India Company at Poplar and the proposed St. Martin-in-the-Fields orchestra premises in Shadwell will in different ways demonstrate the enormous draw which history and architecture have for the public. The riverside pubs have already shown this, particularly those with an historic ambience.

Heritage Trails

For many potential visitors to the area, however, Docklands will be a new experience. Its heritage has been unsung or inaccessible for many years, and few guide books to London cover the area in any detail.

The Corporation therefore intends to publish a series of Heritage Trails, describing walks and routes which take in historic features and giving descriptions and brief histories. The first Heritage Trail, covering the Isle of Dogs, has already been published. Eight others are so far planned for publication: the River Heritage Route to Greenwich, the Docklands Railway Heritage Route, and Heritage Trails in Poplar, Limehouse, Wapping, Tooley Street and St. Saviour's Dock, Rotherhithe and the Royal Docks.

Most of these Trails will cover areas which can easily be walked – especially once the new railway and river boat services come into operation to provide ready access. In the case of areas such as the Royal Docks, where the distances are considerable, road transport or access via the famous free Woolwich Ferry might be required, though the intended extension of the Docklands Railway to the Royal Docks and Beckton will provide intermediate stations with which the Trails there could connect.

Museums

Museums present the best opportunity for many people – old and young alike – to discover and enjoy their heritage. Whilst the LDDC's principal concern is to ensure the conservation of the Docklands heritage within the regeneration of the area, it realises that attractively organised museums can provide a valuable educational resource and be a great visitor attraction. Indeed, the variety of the heritage has itself created interest in the establishment of a number of new museums in the area and in the refurbishment of others.

The Passmore Edwards Museum, which has shown inventiveness and imagination and an acute sense for exploiting opportunities, has already been given considerable support by the LDDC for its two projects in Newham – the former North Woolwich Railway Station, now restored by the Corporation and adapted to form a museum of the old Great Eastern Railway, and St. Mark's Church, Silvertown, which is to be adapted to form a Museum of Victorian Life.

The National Museum of Labour History is currently located in the old Limehouse Town Hall, a listed building near St. Anne's Church, Limehouse. The museum is hoping to develop new premises that will enable it to display its large collection of trade union banners, though better display techniques might make it unnecessary for them to move from their present premises. The Metropolitan Police also have a small museum in Docklands, and are giving consideration to the location of a major collection in Wapping. There have been approaches by other museum organisations too. These include the National Maritime Museum, which has expressed the wish to establish a boat museum on the Isle of Dogs, and there is talk of a museum of religious history

to be located in St. George-in-the-East in Wapping.

However the largest museum project being assisted by the Corporation is the proposed new Museum of Docklands, which the Museum of London is working to set up. The Museum has been actively involved (in conjunction with the Port of London Authority) in collecting artefacts from the docks for over fifteen years and now has a considerable collection. It also has a unique collection of material relating to London's old industries, including a series of complete trade workshops, which is at present in store in a restored, listed warehouse in the Royal Victoria Dock. The Corporation has made further space available in an adjoining warehouse for the larger artefacts in the collection, and has purchased for the museum a small steam tug – the 'Knocker White' – which will ultimately be displayed in the Docklands Museum.

The scale of this collection renders it of great importance as a record of London as a port. Because of this, the LDDC has provided assistance with its conservation and preparation for eventual display. To help speed up progress, a Manpower Services Commission team has been set up to carry out conservation work under the direction of museum staff, whilst the LDDC is promoting a trust for a Museum in Docklands to take over the management of the collection and set up and run the museum. It is also preparing a graphic history of Docklands from the splendid material in the archives of the PLA now in the Museum of London's care.

It had been hoped that the new museum would be located within and form an important part of the Port East tourist development on the North Quay of the West India Import Dock. However, it seems more and more unlikely that this can be achieved and an alternative site is being actively sought. It is nevertheless hoped that it will be possible for the museum to establish a presence there: with a small gallery and part of the quayside to show cargo handling and with displays of floating exhibits in the adjacent dock it could be an important draw, even if the main museum were not located there.

'W' Warehouse, Royal Victoria Dock

North Woolwich Railway Museum

North Woolwich Railway Museum

The 'John W Mackay'

The 'Golden Hind'

The capital costs involved in setting up the museum will obviously be substantial and, although the Corporation would endeavour to make a substantial contribution, there will clearly have to be major funding from other sources. There is great potential for raising sponsorship for a project of this kind and the museum will need to make a great effort in this direction.

Such schemes apart, it must be remembered that Docklands, especially in its historic buildings, engineering artefacts and industrial archaeology, is itself a living museum of Britain's rise to industrial greatness and her maritime power. Many of the historical artefacts of Docklands are in situ – either on the ground or in the water. What is most needed here is a modest initial provision for a Docklands History Interpretation Centre, which would house special small exhibitions, run the Heritage Trails and provide a source of information about Docklands' history. The establishment of such a centre could represent a valuable first step towards serving the growing public interest in Docklands' history, its architecture, archaeology and its artefacts.

Historic Ships

Docklands has played a major part in the maritime history of Britain. Within it lies the shipyard that built most of the ships for the Royal Navy in the 18th Century; another Docklands yard built the largest vessel of its day in the 19th Century. On both sides of the Thames the whole life of the community was dependent on shipping. It is therefore appropriate that the Corporation should give attention to attracting historic ships to Docklands today.

Sadly, there are now few preserved large square riggers requiring a home. Most are moored in the many ports in America that are undergoing regeneration: those that remain are generally in poor condition and in remote places, and the cost of bringing them back to England and restoring them would be considerable. Such a move would only be feasible if private individuals or wealthy

foundations could provide the financial resources. Nevertheless, the LDDC is looking into the possibility of assisting one suitable trust which owns an important square rigged vessel with its restoration, in return for its display in the West India Docks.

There are, however, many smaller sailing vessels that are actually still in use, earning a living by doing charter work and film work, and many of these need a home base from which to sail. The West India Docks have provided a convenient base for several vessels in the past, and the Corporation has encouraged this use by offering preferential mooring rates. Many Thames sailing barges have also been preserved, and it is hoped that several of these can be berthed in the West India Docks. As their masts can be lowered they can be taken under the bridges so there will be many more places available to berth them. Their attractive lines and relatively small size should appeal to owners of quayside buildings, whom it is hoped will co-operate with the LDDC in making berths available.

One ship preservation project to which the Corporation has given active support is that of the 'John W Mackay'. Probably the oldest steam driven cableship in the world, the ship still contains its steam driven machinery. Its cabins, ranging from the beautifully panelled master's day cabin and officers' saloon to the spartan quarters of the ordinary seamen, still retain their original fittings. Galleys, stores, workshops and test laboratories all remain. With this raw material it will be possible to tell in a dramatic way the story of life at sea in the earlier part of this century, and to show the development of the telecommunications industry, now playing such an important part in the regeneration of present-day Docklands. It is hoped that the 'John W Mackay' will be permanently moored in the West India Docks where it is currently berthed, or else in the Royal Docks, to contribute to the development of tourist attractions.

The mooring of a good variety of historic ships within the docks will have considerable visual appeal, and the continual changing of the smaller vessels will create life and activity along the quaysides – as is already evident at the St. Katharine Docks. It is hoped that a display of historic ships will be mounted in the West India Import Dock, in conjunction with the planned shore-side leisure facilities there. The Maritime Trust has a good collection and the LDDC will be seeking to come to an agreement in the future for the display of some of these.

At the same time it is the Corporation's policy to encourage owners of suitable historic vessels to moor them in the West India Docks. The replica 'Godspeed' received a send-off to Virginia from Island Gardens and that of Francis Drake's 'Golden Hind' was berthed in West India Dock as were the 'Winston Churchill' and a number of other historic sailing ships. The famous tea clipper, the 'Cutty Sark', is permanently in dry dock at Greenwich opposite Island Gardens.

Large parts of the West India Docks are unfortunately inaccessible to large ships because of the 8 metre air draught between water level and the Docklands Light Railway viaduct. The pace of development also means that there will be almost no lengths of quay in LDDC ownership available for moorings until development is complete, although some provision has been made for ships making short term visits. On quayside sites where the Corporation is no longer in control, vessel owners will need to make arrangements direct with developers, though if both site and vessel are suitable the Corporation would support negotiations.

The question of suitable historic ship moorings in the Royal Docks has yet to be resolved. This will depend on whether the lock can remain operational and, in the case of the Royal Victoria Dock, whether opening bridges are provided at the Connaught Passage.

Archaeology

Large parts of Docklands were virtually uninhabited until comparatively recently, and it is not especially likely, therefore, that archaeological remains will be found.

However, an exciting discovery has been made at Bermondsey, and there is evidence of early settlements at various points along the banks of the Thames. It is important to the understanding of the history of London that the remains of these settlements are investigated before they are destroyed by the extensive substructure work of new development. This has been done on the site of the Royal Mint, where the remains of a Cistercian Monastery have been discovered: they will be on permanent display as part of the redevelopment scheme.

There are also remains from the Roman era. The site of a Roman signal station was found a few years ago in Wapping beside The Highway and this, together with Roman burials in the area, indicates that The Highway was probably a Roman road. It leads from London eastwards in the direction of Free Trade Wharf. As this latter site was situated on a gravel outcrop, the first area of firm ground below London, there has been considerable speculation that there might have been a Roman deep water port at that point. Clearly, if a Roman deep water port were to be found there, it would completely alter our understanding of Roman London.

The redevelopment of the Free Trade Wharf site presented a good opportunity for an archaeological dig. Sadly, the trial dig carried out by the Greater London Archaeological Unit following discussions with the developer found no evidence that would substantiate the existence of a port. As there were deep basements on the site any remains (if indeed they ever existed) could, however, have been destroyed when the basements were built. The river frontage may also have moved either way, and the Roman river wall could lie under the road or have been eroded away by the river. We will probably never know.

An excavation at Fennings Wharf, next to London Bridge, uncovered the remains of one of the 'starlings' of Old London Bridge. This dig was mostly financed by the developer, although the Corporation made a small contribution.

Cranes in the West India Docks

Museum in Docklands

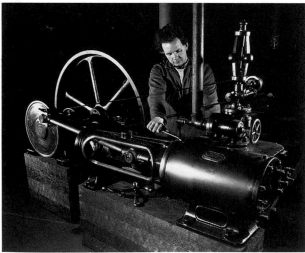

Museum in Docklands

Normally, archaeological digs on sites in Docklands would not be expected to reveal any major remains – certainly not ones that would justify scheduling as Ancient Monuments – and the sites would, after investigation, be developed in the normal way. However, on the Cherry Garden, Bermondsey site the exceptional has been found in the shape of what is almost certainly the remains of Edward III's residence. Although lost for centuries, its existence in Rotherhithe had been known from original building accounts, which described it as a large stone moated house with two courtyards.

The remains found on the initial trial excavation are impressive in scale and are well preserved. The Corporation has funded a further and more detailed investigation which has indicated that a considerable proportion of the lower part of the building has survived, and that at the very least a full scale excavation should be carried out. The Corporation is now looking into the possibility of these remains being conserved and displayed to the public, and taken into the guardianship of English Heritage.

This find ranks among one of the most important in the country during this decade. There will doubtless be a great deal of interest in it, particularly on the part of tourists, who already come to Rotherhithe to visit The Mayflower public house, St. Mary's School and the Brunel Engine House. It will also be a valuable educational facility, giving local children a sense of the history on their doorstep.

Such dramatic discoveries cannot be expected to occur very frequently: archaeology in Docklands is more likely to be a low-key, unglamorous affair, in which sites will be carefully recorded and then left for development. Such painstaking work is currently being undertaken in Southwark where, in order to establish the location of remains on the many Corporation-owned sites, the Corporation is helping to fund archival research by a topographical study to reveal the most likely sites of early settlements and those most likely to be productive. Trial digs will be carried out in appropriate cases to see if the site is worth investigating further, although whether such digs can take place will depend upon the strength of the evidence, and the pace of development which the LDDC, under its remit from Government, is required to achieve.

The Corporation cannot itself support the financing of any large scale site digs. Developers will, however, be encouraged to assist archaeologists by making sites available for digs before development takes place, as is frequently done in the City of London. The LDDC will support archaeologists if they are willing and able to keep to agreed programmes: if the dig is not finished within agreed time limits, it has to be left.

It is perhaps in the field of industrial archaeology that Docklands will have a special role. At Masthouse Terrace on the south west riverside of the Isle of Dogs part of the original launching slip of Brunel's 'Great Eastern Steamship' has been discovered by the LDDC. The original timber slips are being impregnated and preserved. A vast number of artefacts from the docks has also been rescued, and the Museum of London has been in the forefront of collecting and restoring them. The LDDC has assisted financially and has restored 'W' warehouse in the Royal Victoria Dock as a store, restoration workshop and visitor centre operated by the Museum. As has already been mentioned, a special team funded by the Manpower Services Commission, which has already carried out some excellent work, is engaged on a two year programme of restoration of artefacts, bringing many into working condition, thus providing employment and training, and developing an invaluable enterprise in restoration techniques. 'W' warehouse is probably the last remaining warehouse to be restored to its original form, and as such provides the ultimate artefact of the Museum in Docklands.

The Corporation has itself set an example through the purchase and restoration of cranes, bridges and other artefacts, some of which (especially the bridges) have been incorporated in regeneration schemes.

The Natural Ecology

The urban fabric which has been created by riverside wharves, quays and jetties, by mudchutes and the impounded water areas of the enclosed docks, has given Docklands its exceptional water-based identity. Less readily observable and therefore less widely appreciated is the unique urban ecology that exists. It contains habitats in, on and around buildings, dock structures and artefacts, and some areas containing substantial vegetation. Even the name Heron Quays in the West India Docks came from observation of these elegant birds, whose habit it was to fish for eels from the bollards on the wharf.

Such habitats are relevant conservation considerations, since they are important products of local history and enable community enjoyment of nature in a developed urban area. They provide expression today in some aspects of Docklands life such as the Mudchute Farm run by the Association of Island Communities on the Isle of Dogs, the similar (though somewhat smaller) Surrey Docks Farm on the opposite side of the river, and more especially in the research and educational role of the ecology park run by The Trust for Urban Ecology in the Surrey Docks redevelopment.

It has been shown along Britain's motorways how unshaven verges can quickly become colonised by wild life. In Docklands, the 'Beckton Alps,' shaped from the capped polluted spoil from an old gas works, may offer the opportunity for some similar form of wild life colonisation. So may the raised banks of the River Lea, where an area is being considered for protection, and the raised woodland-planted escarpment of the proposed East London River Crossing.

Such new habitats for the co-existence of wild life with man may provide important lessons for urban planners. It is hoped that the work of The Urban Ecology Trust in Docklands will be followed with interest by the local communities in Docklands, as well as by local authorities an ' development corporations in other parts of Britain.

The regeneration of London Docklands is one of the largest, and most exciting examples of urban regeneration in the world. Much of the Corporation's work will be watched with interest by those involved in other regeneration projects – not only in Britain, but also in Europe – for many years to come. It is therefore doubly important that conservation should be seen to be playing a constructive role in its activities. The Corporation's principal concern, however, is the successful regeneration of London Docklands itself – and to ensure that innovation, change and the challenge of the new is woven inextricably with the best of the past to create in London Docklands a 'unique place' for residents and visitors alike.

Lavender Pond

The Beckton Alps

Mudchute, Isle of Dogs

London Docklands looking east

Appendix 1
Grants for Historic Buildings and Conservation

There are three types of grant aid for historic buildings and areas available from Government sources. These are:

> **Historic Buildings Grants**
> (Section 3A Grants)
> **Conservation Grants**
> (Section 10 Grants)
> **Town Scheme Grants**
> (Section 10 Grants)

In addition, the London Docklands Development Corporation is empowered to provide listed building grants for specific projects in its conservation areas, and has itself funded a major programme of restoration work.

Historic Buildings Grants

English Heritage (The Historic Buildings and Monuments Commission) is empowered to make Section 3A Grants for repairs to buildings of outstanding historic and architectural interest. These grants form part of a national scheme and are only available for buildings designated as 'outstanding' by the Commission, usually those of Grade I and II* quality. Grant aid is only available for major structural repairs, and is typically made at 40% of the cost of works. It will only be given if the owner cannot otherwise afford the cost of the necessary work. In practice, even if the severe criteria for Section 3A Grants are met, building owners will not receive grant as of right, as the amount of money available to the Commission is limited. A special scheme is operated under Section 3A for 'Churches in Use.'

English Heritage also operates a special scheme of London Grants, introduced in 1986 to replace the scheme formerly operated by the GLC. London Grants are made for the repair and restoration of listed historic buildings, usually Grade II or II* buildings not eligible for Section 3A Grants.

The local authorities are also empowered under the Local Authorities (Historic Buildings) Act 1962 to make grants for historic buildings. They are not so restricted as to criteria as is the Commission, but there are always more demands made on them than they have the money to support. Similarly, the LDDC is empowered to make grants to private individuals and to local authorities for the repair and restoration of historic buildings.

The Department of the Environment will not approve proposals for grant aid from two government sources for any one project – e.g. from both English Heritage and the LDDC. Such 'double granting', as it is called, is not permitted for the same building unless the grants are being made available for quite different aspects of work.

Conservation Grants

Section 10 of the Town and Country Planning (Amendment) Act 1972 (as amended by the Local Government, Planning and Land Act 1980) gives power to operate two separate grant schemes in conservation areas – Conservation Grants and Town Scheme Grants.

Section 10 Grants may be made by the Historic Buildings and Monuments Commission (English Heritage) for any work which makes a *significant contribution towards preserving or enhancing the character or appearance of a conservation area*'. In the past, conservation areas deemed suitable for grant aid have had to be designated as 'outstanding': there are a number of these in Docklands.

Under the terms of the enabling legislation, Section 10 Grants could theoretically be made for any building in any conservation area. However, as funds were (and still are) limited, guidelines for their use were drawn up by the Department of the Environment with the advice of the Historic Buildings Council (the forerunner to English Heritage) and published in 1981 to indicate the type of project likely to be acceptable for grant aid. English Heritage has since adopted these policy guidelines, which aim to ensure that grants are concentrated within defined areas and not scattered so widely that their contribution to the conservation area as a whole is fragmented.

The standard rate of Section 10 Grants within a conservation scheme is 25%, though this is subject to variation in case of need. Since Section 10 Grants are for works to enhance the character or appearance of a conservation area, only structural repairs and external works are eligible. The buildings for which grant aid is typically sought are normally visible from the street, and therefore no requirement is made for public access.

Conservation Grants are also made for environmental improvements such as roads and paths, walls, landscaping, removal of overhead wires, street furniture, etc. Such grants are normally – though not always – made directly to the local or other public authority in the area concerned. The LDDC does not qualify for this kind of grant aid.

Town Scheme Grants

Section 10 Town Scheme Grants are made in cases where English Heritage and a local authority jointly agree to contribute towards repairs to specified buildings within one or more conservation areas in a town. The LDDC is not empowered to enter into such schemes. Grants are made only where the area to be covered by the Town Scheme qualifies on merit as having definite townscape value. In the past, the normal rate of grant has been 25% Commission/25% local authority. In the view of English Heritage, Town Schemes have proved a particularly effective way of stimulating local interest and upgrading limited and defined areas.

LDDC Historic Building and Conservation Grants

The LDDC's Corporate Plan (published annually) sets out the Corporation's environmental policies and programmes.

The Corporation makes listed building grants towards the renovation and adaptation of buildings of special architectural and historic interest and of buildings in Docklands conservation areas. The Corporation is required to ensure that works for which grant application is made contribute to regeneration, and that any contribution towards expenditure incurred by others is consistent with the guidance and criteria issued by the Department of the Environment on historic buildings and conservation.

Corporation funding has for the most part taken the form of large grants to major schemes on premises owned either by private or corporate bodies or by one or other of the Borough Councils, and to schemes on premises which the Corporation itself owns. To date, the Corporation has spent some £4.5 million on listed building works and some £1.5 million on environmental improvements in conservation areas. Proposals for future expenditure in these two areas currently amount to around £10 million. Many of the schemes which the LDDC has funded, or to which it has made grant contributions, are described elsewhere in this publication.

The Corporation has also handled a small

Appendix 2
Article 4 Directions

number of modest applications for improvements to domestic premises, although since there are only a small number of historic residential areas in Docklands (as is reflected in the nature of the designated conservation areas) there are few domestic buildings eligible for grant. Exceptions to this are likely to be in the St. Matthias, All Saints, Wilson Grove and Chapel House Conservation Areas, and a small contingency fund has been established for such purposes.

In addition, there is provision under the Inner Urban Areas Act for grants to be made to encourage commercial firms to develop and expand in inner urban areas. The grants are available specifically within Improvement Areas and apply to environmental improvements and to works to correct or improve buildings for industrial or commercial use.

In its early years, when property values were rising more slowly than they are now, the Corporation made no requirement for recipients of grant to pay back any proportion of the grant if a building was improved and then sold. It was recently decided to apply such a condition if the property on which works have been carried out using grant is sold within 3 years.

Article 3 of the General Development Order 1973 permits certain types of development to be carried out without the permission of the local planning authority. These include alterations to the exterior of dwellings such as changing windows, adding porches and altering external wall finishes. Generally, the Corporation would not wish to interfere with people's rights to do this.

However, there are groups of houses which, while not perhaps of that special quality that would justify listing, do have distinct and interesting character that is worth conserving – character which can so easily be lost if a handful of owners within the group carry out insensitive alterations such as cladding with artificial stone or changing windows. In cases where the Corporation is concerned to ensure that the character of such houses is retained, it will consider the application of Article 4 directions, which remove the rights given in Article 3. These directions will be limited to the minimum required for the retention of the integrity of the group, and will generally only apply to front elevations. Article 4 directions come into force immediately after they have been approved by the Corporation, but need to be confirmed by the Secretary of State within six months.

Whenever Article 4 directions are applied, the Corporation will carry out extensive consultation with house owners and occupiers to try to gain their support: the directions are intended after all to safeguard the majority of owners against the unthoughtful work of one, who may deleteriously affect the overall character of the group by making unsympathetic alterations. Nevertheless, it is clearly sensible to carry out such consultations after the imposition of the Article 4 directions to ensure that deleterious alterations are not

carried out while consultation is taking place.

The imposition of Article 4 directions could result in an increase in the cost of repairs: permission may, for example, be refused for the use of certain materials or workmanship; purpose-made windows might be required instead of standard windows, or slates instead of concrete tiles. In such cases the Corporation will consider making grants towards the difference in costs incurred.

Appendix 3
Repairs Notices and Section 101 Notices

Generally speaking, the LDDC's approach to conservation and historic buildings in Docklands is popular with owners anxious to bring historic buildings back into use as there are clear economic advantages in their doing so. However, there are cases where important historic buildings are neglected by their owners, and are left to decay.

In circumstances where reasonable steps are not being taken properly to preserve a listed building, the Corporation has powers, under the Town and Country Planning Act of 1971, to issue a repairs notice requiring the owner to carry out necessary works. If the owner takes no action within two months, the Corporation can apply to the Department of the Environment for authority to proceed with compulsory purchase. The owner can apply to a Magistrate's Court within 28 days of service of notice for a notice staying compulsory purchase action on the grounds that reasonable steps are being taken to preserve the building.

If the building is unoccupied, the Corporation is empowered under Section 101 of the 1971 Act, after giving seven days notice, to carry out works that are urgently needed for the preservation of a listed building. The costs incurred are recoverable from the owner who has a right of appeal to the Secretary of State.

These are important powers which will enable the Corporation to ensure that listed buildings will not be left to decay, and it should be stressed that the Corporation will use these powers if necessary: derelict buildings present a bad image and hinder regeneration. In the more developed parts of Docklands, such as Wapping or Southwark, the Corporation would generally tend to favour the issue of a repairs notice. If an owner in these areas does not carry out the necessary repairs the building would be compulsorily purchased by the Corporation and passed on to a developer with a commitment to bring it back into use. In the case of buildings for which alternative uses cannot be identified due to their location the Section 101 notice may be more appropriate, the main need here being to prevent further decay until such time as new infrastructure and development make their conversion to new uses viable.

Many of the historic sites and features of architectural interest in Docklands are located on conservation area maps on pages 44-70. Other locations and features of interest mentioned in the text, particularly those in areas which the LDDC is considering for possible listing, are to be found on the 4 area maps which follow.

Wapping and Limehouse

1. London Docks
2. Raine Street
3. Arbour Square (not in the LDDC area)
4. Butcher Row
5. St. Katharine's Foundation
6. Limehouse Kiln

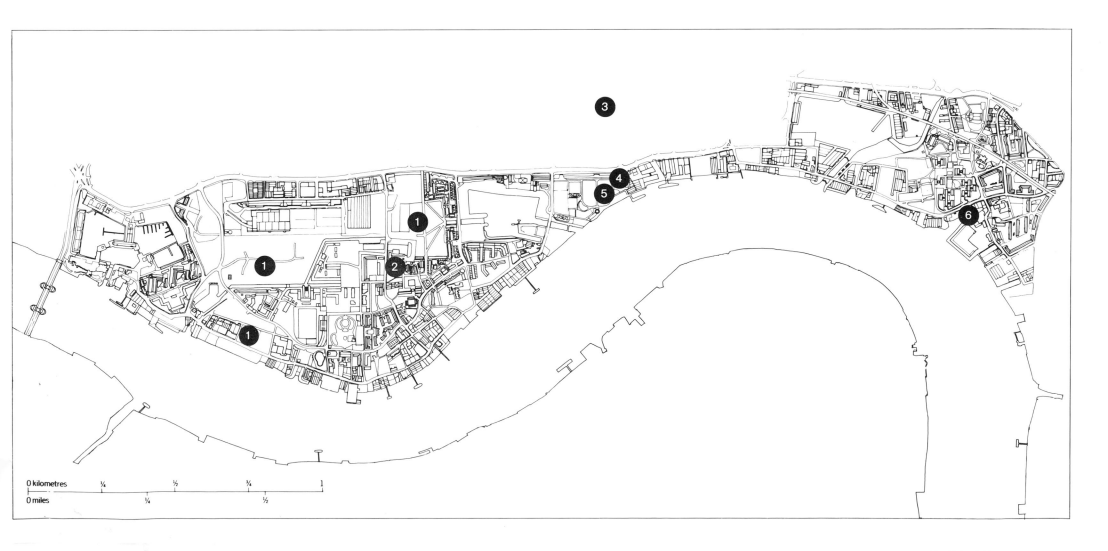

0 kilometres ¼ ½ ¾ 1

0 miles ¼ ½

Surrey Docks

1. Emblem House, Tooley Street
2. No.3 Vine Lane
3. South London College, Bermondsey
4. The Angel
5. St. Olav's Church
6. Former Dock Manager's Office, Surrey Docks
7. Lavender Lock
8. Lavender Pond
9. The Blacksmith's Arms
10. Columbia Wharf
11. Nelson House, Rotherhithe
12. Nelson Dockyard
13. Surrey Docks Farm
14. Church House/Bryan House
15. Holy Trinity Church
16. Acorn Estate
17. Canada Wharf
18. St. James Church, Bermondsey
19. Finnish Seamen's Church

0 kilometres ½ 1

0 miles ¼ ½

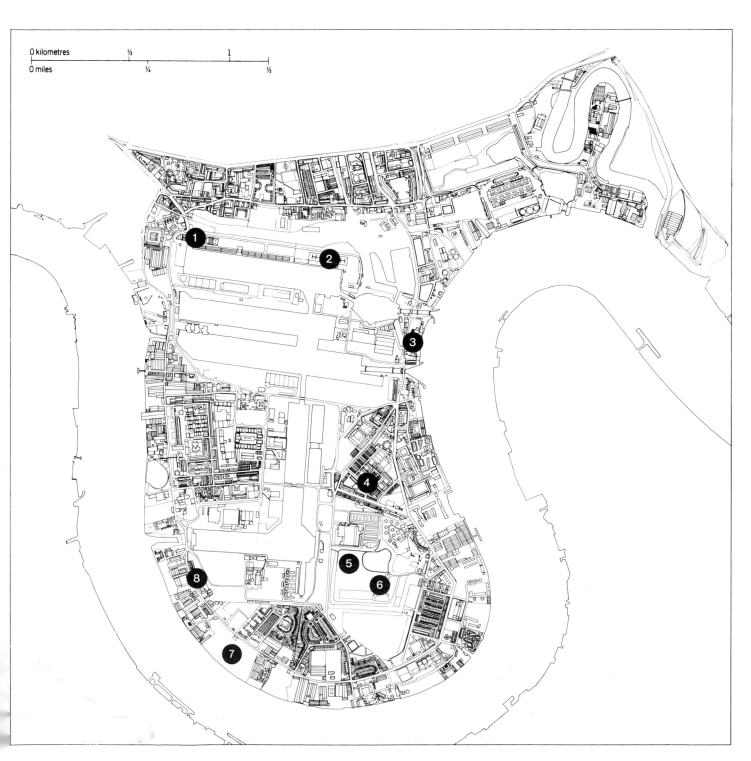

Isle of Dogs

1. Port East
2. Billingsgate Fish Market
3. River Police Station Coldharbour
4. Strattondale Street
5. Mudchute
6. Mudchute Farm
7. Napier Yard
8. St. Paul's Presbyterian Church

0 kilometres ½ 1

0 miles ¼ ½

Royal Docks

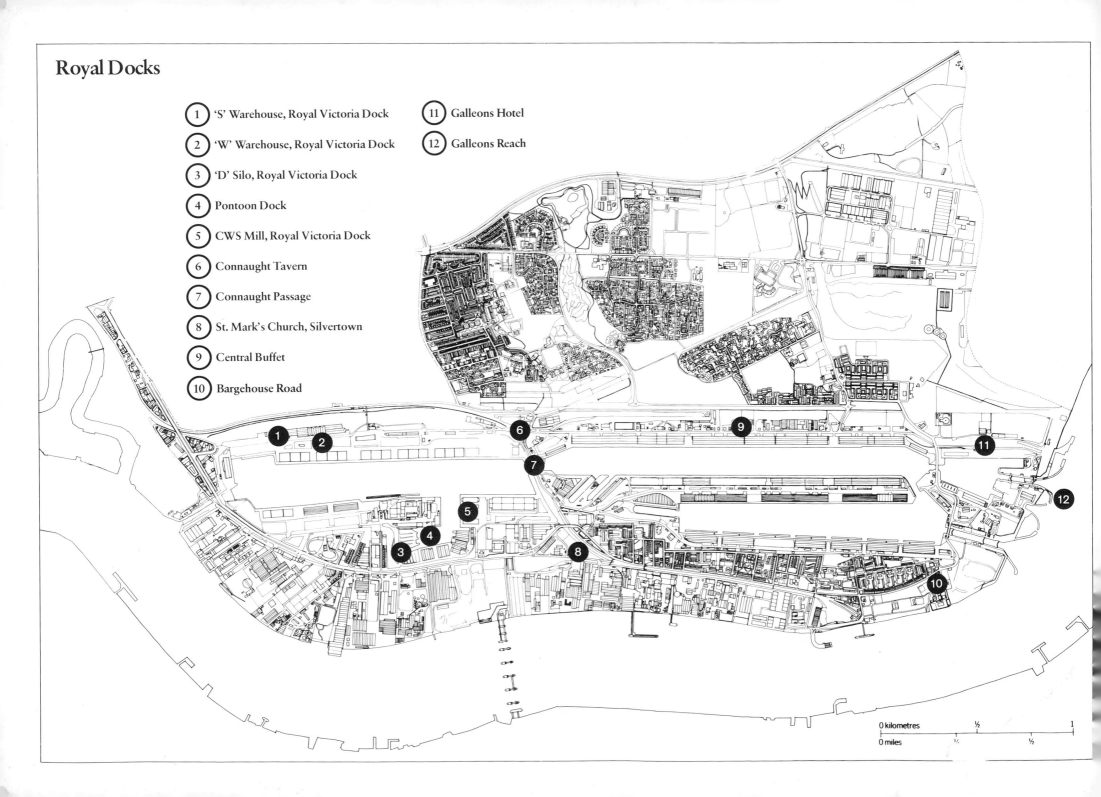

1. 'S' Warehouse, Royal Victoria Dock
2. 'W' Warehouse, Royal Victoria Dock
3. 'D' Silo, Royal Victoria Dock
4. Pontoon Dock
5. CWS Mill, Royal Victoria Dock
6. Connaught Tavern
7. Connaught Passage
8. St. Mark's Church, Silvertown
9. Central Buffet
10. Bargehouse Road

11. Galleons Hotel
12. Galleons Reach

0 kilometres ½ 1
0 miles ¼ ½

Acknowledgements

The Editors and Publishers are grateful to the following people for their permission to reproduce photographs and drawings.

Dust jacket illustration of Tobacco Dock by Terry Farrell Partnership
Page vi, Wyngaerd 'Panorama' of 1543 from the Port of London Authority Collection, Museum of Docklands.
Page viii, Hogarth's Idle Prentice from the Port of London Authority Collection, Museum of Docklands.
Page xi, John Fairburn's plan of West India Dock from the Port of London Authority Collection, Museum of Docklands.
Page xii, Stanford's map of London, 1865, from the Robert Clarke Collection.
Page 1, The Crown Estate Commissioners.
Page 2, London Borough of Tower Hamlets Central Library.
Page 3, The Imperial War Museum.
Page 5, Canaletto's 'View of Greenwich Palace,' reproduced by kind permission of the Trustees of the National Maritime Museum.
Page 6, Tantrums (Keith Gilbert and Jack Hough).
Page 11, Martin Charles.
Page 13, Roof trusses, Tantrums (Keith Gilbert and Jack Hough).
Page 16, St. Patrick's Church altar, Tantrums (Keith Gilbert and Jack Hough).
Page 18, St. Mark's Church during reconstruction, David Tedman.
Page 20, Watercolour of St. Matthias Church from the Port of London Authority Collection, Museum in Docklands.
Page 21, St. Matthias Church present condition and ceiling boss, S.A. Ringer; Pastel drawing of the Baroque opera, Keith Harrison Associates drawn by Robin Linklater.
Page 24, Drawing of vacuum pump, The Art Company.
Page 26, Tobacco Dock vaults, Steve Theodorou for Architects Journal.
Page 29, Boilerhouse, Pollard Thomas

Edwards; Reconstruction drawing by Donald Insall.
Page 30, Free Trade Wharf, drawings by Holder and Matthias Partnership.
Page 31, Thames Tunnel Mills atrium and window detail, David Tedman.
Page 32, Hays Galleria under construction and view across river by Reg Perkes; Galleria drawing by Michael Twigg Brown and Partners.
Page 33, Drawings of Wapping Pumping Station, Arup Associates Architects & Engineers & Quantity Surveyors, Arup Acoustics: Acousticians.
Page 35, The 'Great Eastern Steamship,' from the Port of London Authority Collection, Museum in Docklands.
Page 36, Poplar Town Hall, Graham Challifour.
Page 37, Poplar Technical College, Graham Challifour.
Page 38, Former St. Olave's Grammar School, Martin Charles; 18c Schoolhouse, Rotherhithe, Vernon Gibbard Associates
Page 39, The Prospect of Whitby, Jo Reid and John Peck.
Page 40, Wapping Pierhead, Edward Sargent; Window detail, David Tedman; Newell Street, Tantrums (Jack Hough).
Page 42, Rum Warehouses, Deptford, Graham Challifour; Abbey of St. Mary Graces excavation drawing, Gordon Cullen.
Page 43, Matthew Whiting's House and Wall Paintings, Tantrums (Keith Gilbert and Jack Hough).
Pages 44 and 45, Island Design.
Pages 47, 53 and 55, Handford Photography.
Page 61, Narrow Street, Peter Cook.
Page 62, Engraving of Milligan Statue from the Port of London Authority Collection, Museum of London.
Page 63, Photograph of West India Dock Gateway from the Port of London Authority Collection, Museum of London; Illustration of Port East, Fitch and Co.
Page 69, All Saints Church Rectory and Montague Place, Dawn Tebutt.

Page 70, East India Dock Wall, Tantrums (Jack Hough).
Page 71, St. Olaf's House, Tooley Street, Tantrums (Keith Gilbert and Jack Hough).
Page 74, St. Katharine Docks, Martin Charles; Tobacco Dock illustration, Terry Farrell Partnership; St. Matthias Church, Keith Harris Associates drawn by Robin Linklater; Railway viaduct over West India Dock, Gordon Cullen.
Page 75, 'W' Warehouse, Tantrums (Jack Hough and Keith Gilbert); North Woolwich Railway Museum, David Tedman.
Page 77, Cranes in West India Docks, Alex Bartell.
Page 78, Museum in Docklands from the Port of London Authority Collection, Museum in Docklands.

All other photographs supplied by the Consultant Editor and London Docklands Development Corporation Picture Library.

Index

Figures in bold refer to illustrations, figures in italics are map references. A number of locations are shown on the composite map of London Docklands on pages 44/45; more are shown on individual conservation area maps; the remainder are to be found on the area maps on pages 83 to 86.